Project-Led
Strategic Management

Project-Led Strategic Management

Project Management Solutions to Develop and Implement Strategy

James Marion
John Lewis
Tracey Richardson

BEP

BUSINESS EXPERT PRESS

Leader in applied, concise business books

Project-Led Strategic Management: Project Management Solutions to Develop and Implement Strategy
Copyright © Business Expert Press, LLC, 2021.

First published in 2021 by
Business Expert Press, LLC
222 East 46th Street, New York, NY 10017
www.businessexpertpress.com

ISBN-13: 978-1-95253-889-6 (paperback)
ISBN-13: 978-1-95253-891-9 (e-book)

Business Expert Press Portfolio and Project Management Collection

Collection ISSN: 2156-8189 (print)
Collection ISSN: 2156-8200 (electronic)

Cover image licensed by Ingram Image, StockPhotoSecrets.com
Cover and interior design by S4Carlisle Publishing Services Private Ltd., Chennai, India

First edition: 2021

10 9 8 7 6 5 4 3 2 1

Printed in the United States of America.

Description

Strategic management is very well documented in business books and in the literature, but that does not make the task any easier. Because formulating and implementing strategy is so taxing, and the environmental signals are so intangible, strategic planning is a responsibility that is easy to avoid. To complicate the matter even more, when deciding on an organizational strategy, the well-being of employees, shareholders, and customers is at stake. The solution proposed in this book is a project management framework to advance organizational strategy. Project management has a long success record of organizing the complex, intangible, and high-risk activities associated with planning, developing, and implementing complex systems. In this book, you'll find not only a description of how use the project management framework to advance strategic management, but also a case study that illustrates the positive impact.

Keywords

strategy; project management; governance; knowledge management

Contents

Introduction: Strategy Is Hard

Strategy by far is one of the most difficult activities for the practicing executive. It requires the application of significant brainpower. Strategic thinking can sap the energy from any executive because of the impossible volume of variables to consider. When deciding the strategy of the company, the well-being of employees, shareholders, and customers is at stake. The information considered in strategic planning is often ambiguous and intangible. To make an analogy, consider the example of an airline pilot attempting to follow a course through a violent thunderstorm and monitoring the cockpit dashboard while blindfolded. In spite of the challenge, the difficulty, and the focus required to make strategic decisions, it is the fundamental responsibility of the executive to make those decisions and to frequently course-correct along the way. While doing so, there is always the danger that some tiny detail will be missed, resulting in a failed strategy and undesired outcomes. Because formulating and deciding upon strategy is so taxing and the environmental signals are so intangible, strategic planning is a responsibility that is easy to avoid. It is far easier to simply "do" rather than "think about what to do." This is precisely what some companies do. They try something, and if it works, they do more of it. If it doesn't work, they try something else—wasting time and money along the way (while avoiding the effort of thinking in the process!). In short, nothing is more difficult, challenging, and taxing than taking in the array of environmental signals, analyzing them, thinking deeply about them, and, finally, making the leap from the conceptual to the practical in strategic implementation. Also, because environmental signals and competitor and customer moves occur continuously, it is often unclear when to embark upon the development of strategy or how often to do it. It should be unsurprising then that a taxing responsibility involving multiple variables and intangible and shifting data within unclear time horizons is rarely done well.

What to Do about It...

The proposed antidote for the crushing difficulty associated with strategic planning and implementation is *process* and *structure*. Such an approach offers the possibility of reducing the inherent ambiguity of the effort and reduces the need to think about questions such as "What should the company be doing, why, and when does this need to be decided?"

The intangibility and ambiguity inherent in strategic planning and implementation has parallels in activities such as requirements collection and analysis for software and systems development. Such activities carried out within the realm of information systems are by their nature intangible, often miscommunicated and misunderstood, and often gotten wrong. Software and systems development have gradually improved via the implementation of process and structure. One of the key elements of such structure is the project management framework. Project management has a long success record of organizing the complex, intangible, and high-risk activities associated with planning, developing, and implementing complex systems. What is strategy development but "requirements collection and analysis" for a company—that is implemented through the development of the company "software" of people, processes, communication, and structure?" Could not the close and focused management practices afforded by the same project management processes employed within intangible, software-intensive knowledge work also be applied to executive-level strategic analysis, formulation, and implementation? This book says "yes" and explains how.

PART 1

How Project Management Fits in Strategic Management

Project management has long been viewed through the lens of technical management. From its formal beginnings in Department of Defense projects in the 1950s, project management practices have continued to fill the need for a comprehensive set of processes that aid managers in dealing with the natural complexity associated with product, technology, and systems development. Consistent with this view is the observation that many schools continue to offer project management degree programs from within schools of engineering or information technology. What gets lost in the "project management as technical management" perspective is the natural fit observed between project management practice and the process of strategy formulation and implementation. An understanding and appreciation of this fit may be developed by clarifying how the elements of project management practice align with the generally accepted practices of strategic management. It could be argued that the analysis, formulation, selection, and implementation of strategy are naturally complex in much the same way as technology projects. Strategy is the result of the firm attempting to make sense of the chaotic macroenvironment and to marshal the moving pieces of the company to attain and to maintain a competitive advantage. This complicated effort requires the close management that project management practice can provide (Figure 1).

What Is a Project?

A project, by formal definition, is a temporary endeavor that is unique, has a defined beginning and end, is complex, employs resources, and produces deliverables. Project management is the application of practices

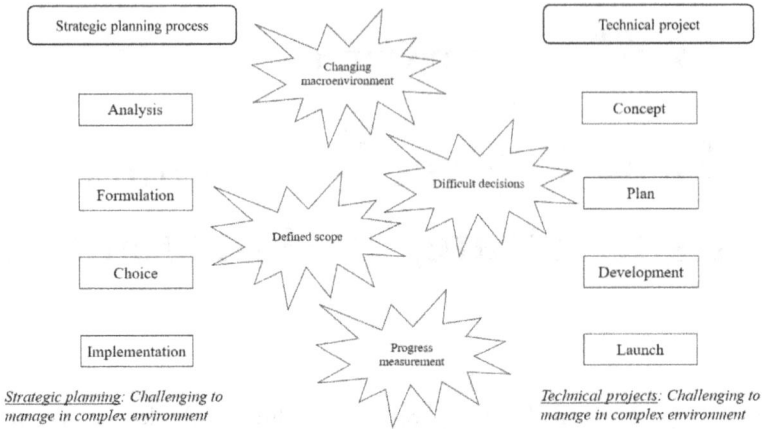

Strategic planning process		Technical project
Analysis	Changing macroenvironment	Concept
Formulation	Difficult decisions	Plan
	Defined scope	
Choice		Development
Implementation	Progress measurement	Launch

Strategic planning: Challenging to manage in complex environment

Technical projects: Challenging to manage in complex environment

Figure 1 Strategic planning versus technical projects

that seek to ensure that the required project deliverables are produced with the appropriate scope, on schedule, and within the constraints of the budget. The simple definitions of project and project management betray little evidence of its historical placement within the domain of R&D and technical management. Yet, the roots of project management are planted firmly where the processes are deemed to pay the largest dividends. The creation of technologically complex deliverables is characterized by a high degree of uncertainty thereby requiring intensive management focus and novel management methodologies. Further, research and development endeavors are often described as exercises in discovery that may fail to converge in the absence of close management. In the information technology domain, software and system development efforts include components that must be identified, specified, developed, and integrated. Such activity occurs in the context of moving targets that take the form of changing standards, shifting client requirements, and intangible work products. It may be argued that a systematic framework of processes created for producing deliverables naturally emerged within environments that included high technical difficulty, complexity, intangibility, and uncertainty. At the same time, it is observed that many other management endeavors can be complex and involve significant uncertainty. Project management therefore has gained a foothold in nontechnical yet complex and uncertain management environments.

The Process of Project Management

The Project Management Institute outlines a set of 49 processes for producing deliverables in the context of a temporary endeavor or project. The processes are organized into five process groups and ten knowledge areas. The process groups are aligned in the simple sequence consisting of initiating, planning, executing, monitoring and controlling, and closing. By inspection, planning, executing, and monitoring and controlling resemble the "Plan-Do-Check" sequence of the Deming Cycle and are likely to be familiar to most managers. The process groups provide an outline of the overall sequence of steps to be carried out throughout a project. Supporting the process groups are the 10 knowledge areas (Figure 2).

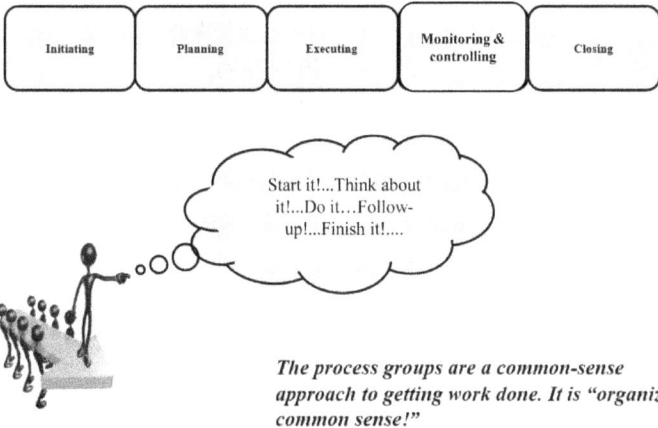

The process groups are a common-sense approach to getting work done. It is "organized common sense!"

Figure 2 The PMBOK process groups

The knowledge areas may be understood as the content view of managing the project. The 10 knowledge areas include integration, scope, time, cost, quality, resources, communication, risk, procurement, and stakeholders (Figure 3).

These knowledge areas outline the skill sets and domain expertise that is to be applied within the five process groups. When project managers apply project management processes, they typically do so in the form of a temporary organization, or project team, that is authorized by executive management. It is of interest to observe that the process group sequence of project management could be said to mirror the series of steps associated with the strategic management process. The benefit of the PMBOK framework in the context of strategic management is that it provides a

The domains of skill and expertise that are employed within the PMBOK process groups!

Coordinate	Integration
What?	Scope
When?	Time
How much?	Cost
How high?	Quality
Who?	Human resources
Report	Comms.
Anticipate	Risk
Outsource	Procure
Collaborate	Stakeholder

Figure 3 The PMBOK knowledge areas

clear-cut starting and ending point for each major activity or set of strategic activities. Because each phase of the strategic management process begins and ends, each phase could be envisioned as projects and managed as such. The project management framework is therefore useful to have at the disposal of management to add structure to strategic activity in a business environment that is continuously changing and fluid (Figure 4).

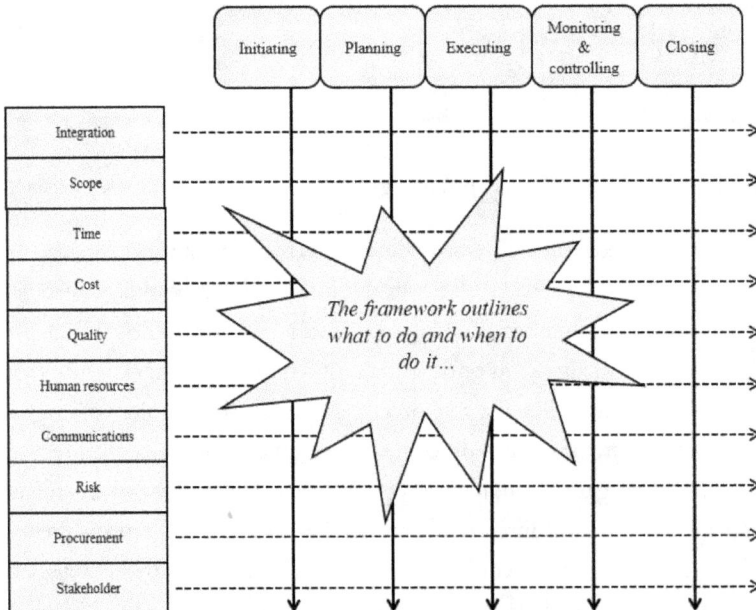

Figure 4 Combining knowledge areas and process groups

Projects and Organizations

Whereas projects exist to deliver the project scope using the project management process framework, the strategic management of the firm sets the direction for an ongoing, continuous operation. The ongoing operation sets its sights on the long term. Instead of a focus on immediate tangible deliverables, ongoing operations seek to carry out the mission and vision of the firm by satisfying customers, shareholders, and stakeholders while seeking to attain and maintain a competitive advantage. Although an ongoing operation is said to be continuous, much of the work done by an operation could be characterized as discrete in nature. For example, firms seeking to carry out a mission and vision do so by delivering products and services of various categories. The development of such products and services may be managed as projects since they are unique, complex, and temporary. The effort to develop a new product or service terminates at market launch. Once the product or service is launched, the operation on a continuous basis satisfies customers by making endless copies of the finished product via its ongoing production operations. To make an analogy, an ongoing operation could be viewed as an ocean liner continuously sailing toward the horizon (Figure 5).

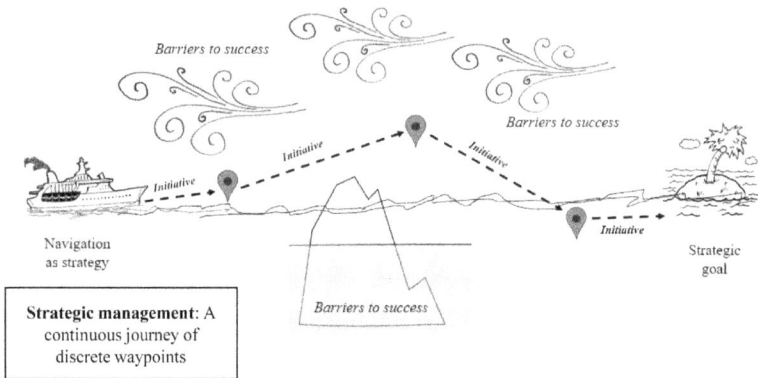

Figure 5 Strategy as steering toward waypoints

Although the path of the ocean liner is continuous, the ship progresses toward the horizon via unique and discrete navigational waypoints. The ship is buffeted by waves, wind, and other unique environmental disturbances. Yet, course corrections are implemented, and risks minimized so that the next milestone is reached. Likewise, in operations, products, services, and other unique and temporary initiatives act as milestones along the way that point toward the ultimate vision and mission horizon. These strategic "waypoints" are managed as discrete bundles of activities and deliverables managed by project managers. Strategic management could therefore be viewed as the ongoing activity of resighting the specific direction on the horizon and taking action to steer the ship. What appears to be continuous involves four discrete activities—each of which includes many subactivities that are designed to answer key questions and take important next steps. The questions are not easy to answer and require close oversight. Further, the "next steps" are likely to involve significant implementation plans. The cluster of strategic activities could be observed to benefit from the employment of project management practices. The discrete activities and subactivities include:

1. Revisiting where the ship needs to go
    a. Are the previous assumptions about direction correct?
    b. Will arrival at the next milestone result in success?
2. Determining where the ship currently is
    a. What is our progress toward the next waypoint?
    b. Are we on course or have we drifted?
3. Resighting the target on the horizon
    a. Is the target still there?
    b. Are the coordinates for attaining the goal correct?
4. Taking action to steer the ship
    a. Have we drifted off course?
    b. Do we need to make adjustments based upon currents, storms, and prevailing winds observed ahead?

Each of these steps is repeated as waypoints are reached or as required adjustments are made.

Strategic Waypoints

The imagery of a ship navigating to discrete waypoints for the purpose of reaching a destination aligns well with the activity of a company plotting and carrying out strategic initiatives. It is observed therefore that the development and implementation of strategy may be conceived as a series of discrete activities that may be managed as projects. Although the refining of strategy often occurs on an annual cycle, the macroenvironment changes as does the internal situation of the business. For this reason, every strategic planning cycle includes elements that are unique. Since the strategic planning process is unique in every planning period, and the activities carried out in each of the strategic planning phases are temporary, often complex, and involve the application of resources, the process of strategic planning is an ideal candidate for the use of project management practices (Figure 6).

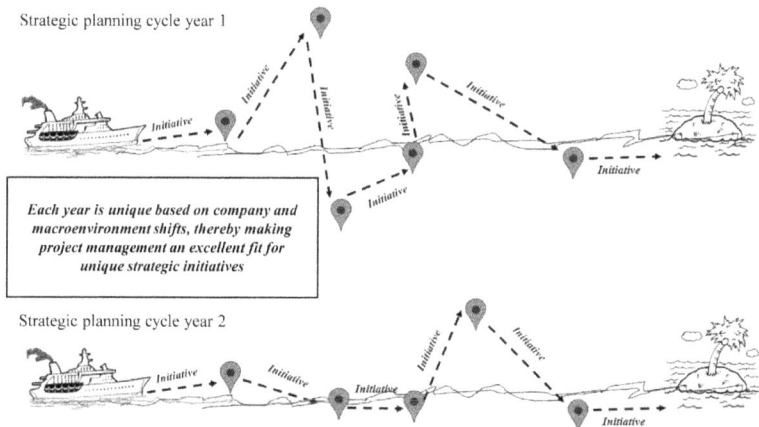

Figure 6 Uniqueness of each strategic planning cycle

Strategy and Strategic Management

Strategy may be described as "making sense of a situation, making choices, making things happen, and making revisions" (Sull 2007). In generic terms, strategy begins with an analysis of the internal and external environment, proceeds with the development or formulation of strategy, and, finally, proceeds to its ultimate implementation. The linear and cascading view of strategy has been debated given the observation that the real-world strategic management process is iterative in nature. The iterative view arises from the recognition that every plan that is implemented faces changing conditions both inside the operation and the macroenvironment. Therefore, while the steps in strategic management are steps that build on each other in a linear fashion, the sequence of steps can be (and often is) repeated in practice (Figure 7).

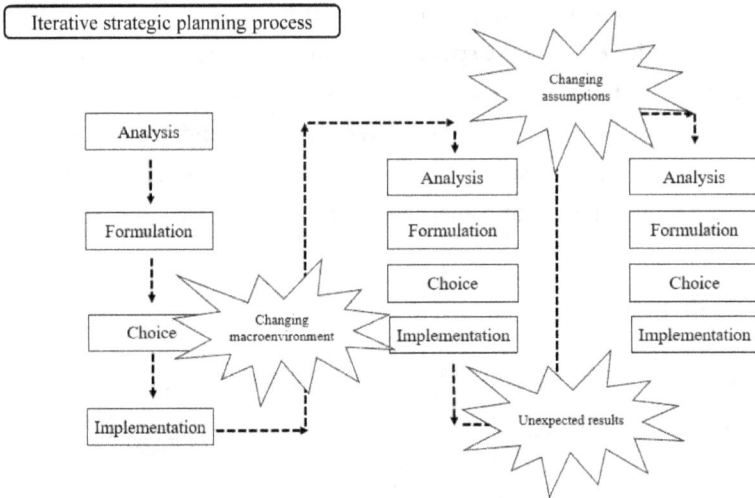

Iterative strategic planning process

| Analysis |
| Formulation |
| Choice |
| Implementation |

Changing macroenvironment

Changing assumptions

| Analysis |
| Formulation |
| Choice |
| Implementation |

| Analysis |
| Formulation |
| Choice |
| Implementation |

Unexpected results

Figure 7 Strategic planning as an iterative process

The linear process of strategy therefore becomes a loop wherein outcomes of implementation are monitored, fed back into the next planning cycle, and used to develop and implement a revised plan. Whether viewed as linear or iterative, strategic management is characterized as a process and managed as such within firms governed by process discipline. Not all companies are observed to have process discipline and may embark upon strategic planning in an ad hoc manner. Such companies may or may not include all steps, and some may approach strategy with intuition rather than process and analysis. Companies that do follow the strategic management process take care to carry out each step. Unlike the continuous ongoing operation that supports the strategic vision, the development of the strategy of the firm as well as the strategic initiatives spawned by the strategic vision are discrete steps. As such, they lend themselves to governance and management as projects since strategy development process actions are unique, have a clear beginning and end, and therefore fit the definition of a project (Figure 8).

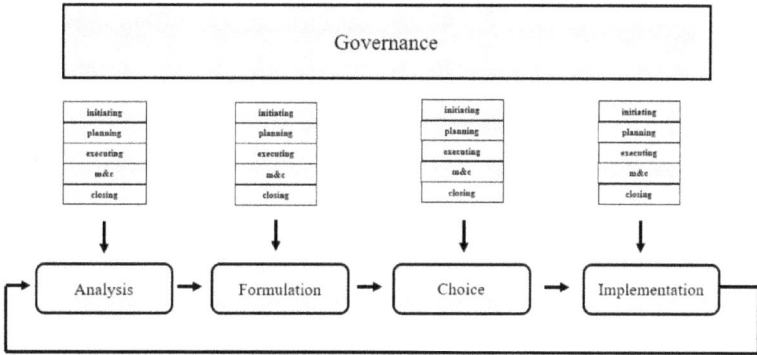

Figure 8 Strategy and governance

CHAPTER 1

Project Management and Strategy Development

Strategy is sometimes thought of as something that emerges from flashes of insight from visionary leaders. While some companies are fortunate to have gifted leaders who can make such conceptual leaps, most are not. Further, visionary strategists are not always right. An alternative approach is to employ repeatable processes that are used to systematically perceive and analyze the macroenvironment and evaluate it considering internal capabilities and know-how. This chapter introduces project management as the fundamental approach to carrying out the development of strategy.

Analysis

Strategic planning begins with analysis. Analysis requires the collection of data, the discussion and review of its implications, and, finally, the organization of the findings so that the organization strengths and weaknesses are characterized. Further, the environment outside of the organization is scrutinized in terms of opportunities and threats. Some firms may dedicate a staff department for periodically carrying out this activity—perhaps within the context of an annual cycle. However, the analysis may or may not always be done formally in organizations. In fact, it is observed that some executives are not able to clearly articulate what the strategy of the company currently is, what it should be, and how it should be developed. Additionally, the deliverables that the process is expected to produce may not always be clearly specified. It is for this reason that project management processes may provide a useful framework for organizing strategic analysis. In project management practice, project teams are formally chartered to create specific deliverables.

The Analysis Challenge

What is it that is analyzed in the development of strategy—and why? The volume of incoming information associated with data analysis is in essence a "big data" problem. Big data in the context of contemporary information technology management is data that is high in volume, that arrives rapidly and often continuously and in real time. Such data is often unstructured. This description of big data aligns well with the volume of information that executives cope within the process of strategic planning. Making sense of so many inputs to the strategic planning is likely to be daunting. Analytics specialists who encounter such data on a daily basis understand that the first step in making headway in understanding the tsunami of data is in arriving at a sound understanding of the problem to be solved. This is a problem of *framing*. Framing a problem correctly allows the decision maker to separate the relevant from the irrelevant and quickly home in on the most important aspects of the data. What problem is it that the executive and associated strategic planning staff seek to solve when carrying out the analysis of the data from the strategic macroenvironment? Simply stated, the company seeks to understand how to attain an "unfair" advantage over the competition—and to sustain it. The word "unfair" is a strong one—but it is one that is appropriate if understood in the strategic planning context (Figure 9).

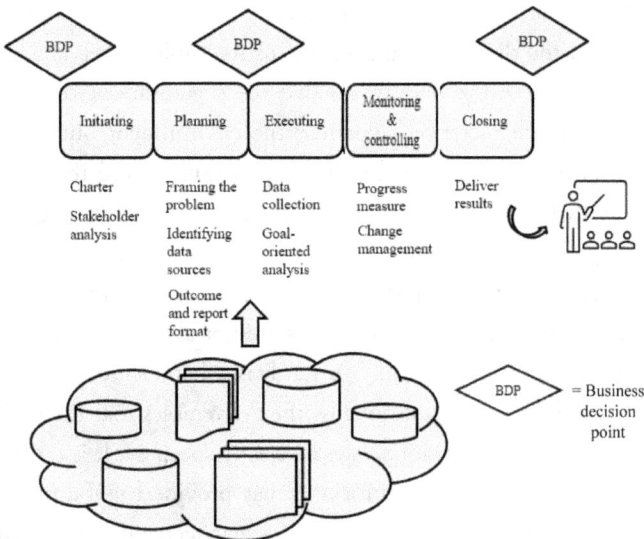

Figure 9 The strategic analysis project

The "Unfair" Advantage

Given the complexity of strategic analysis, it pays to remember that successful strategy development is goal oriented. Rather than being a series of processes that executive teams have to "get through," it has an "endgame" in mind. It is useful therefore to think of the ultimate goal of strategic planning as one of seeking out the means to develop an "unfair" advantage over a competitor. The term "unfair" has the connotation of "having the deck stacked against" the competitor. What does this mean in practice—and why use it? It is because an unfair advantage infers that:

1. The competitor knows what is happening but is unable to succeed at competing against its opponent.
2. The competitor is not able to emulate what the opponent is doing—in spite of being aware of what is happening.
3. In spite of the best efforts of the competitor, the obtained results obtained are substandard.

When a strategy is successful, the "unfair" nature of the competition leads to a situation where the profit that could have been earned by a competitor is instead earned by its opponent in spite of significant effort expended by the competitor. This may ultimately lead to the decline and potential exit of the competitor from the business. Simple examples exist that illustrate the unfair component of strategy.

Example #1: The Housing Crisis of 2007

Consider a homeowner seeking to sell a home at a profit. The homeowner prepares for the sale by updating the kitchen and installing a new roof, windows and doors, and a swimming pool. The owner takes additional steps such as installing a new lawn sprinkler system and planting a garden. The home becomes a true gem and one that is likely to obtain a premium on the housing market. Unfortunately for the homeowner, the home goes on the housing market during the financial collapse of 2007. The home, as beautiful and as well prepared as it is, faces intense competition from thousands of empty homes caught up in foreclosure. Home prices stagnate and fall. The house eventually sells—but at a far lower price than expected. Who earns the profit associated with the increased features and additional work put into the home? It is the buyer rather than the seller. Because of the "unfair advantage" enjoyed by the buyer due to the conditions in the business environment, the buyer has effectively pocketed the profit potential created by the seller.

Example #2: Manufacturer versus Distributor

A typical scenario that unfolds today involves consumer electronics manufacturers seeking to sell their products to major nationwide (and sometimes global) distributors. Because there are many manufacturers competing for the same shelf space—and far more manufacturers than distributors—the retail distributor is in a strong position to demand a specific price level. In spite of the hard work, expended research and development funds, and the building of a brand presence, most consumer electronics manufacturers struggle to achieve high profit margins. Those who do not acquiesce to price demands forfeit shelf space to others waiting in line. Those who do, forfeit the hope of profit margin gains. This is effectively an "unfair" advantage enjoyed by the retailer. The retailer earns the excess profit potential that the manufacturer worked so hard to develop.

Example #3: Amazon versus Local Brick and Mortar

Porter's model suggests that profits are small when competition (i.e., rivalry) is high, and firms have low selling power as well as low buying power. A brick-and-mortar sales operation competes with a company that operates at a far greater scale. The competitor to the brick-and-mortar operation—in this case Amazon—therefore, has high buyer power compared to brick-and-mortar local competition and as a result is able to keep costs low. A consumer considering buying locally is most likely to be "one click away" from a lower price for a product that can usually be delivered overnight. The threat of substitute products is also widely available on the Amazon site and may be easily examined on a smartphone—even while shopping at the brick-and-mortar operation. The scale of Amazon, its buying power, and its access to a wide array of immediately available substitutes earn the company an unfair advantage. As evidence of this, many brick-and-mortar retail operations have exited the market.

In the previous examples, it is observed that the strongest strategy is the unfair advantage and one that is to be sought in strategic analysis.

Military Comparison

A comparison to an army in time of war is a useful way to illustrate analysis within business strategy and competitive advantage. What would be of interest to an army when attempting to gain an "unfair" advantage over the enemy? One of the first elements of analysis is the landscape of the conflict and the position in which the army will occupy. The location of the field of battle is therefore of paramount concern and must be carefully selected after considerable analysis. Why? Because regardless of the capability of the soldiers, a fight is more likely to be successful if the battle is carried out from a strong position—for example—from a hill rather than a valley. The position held within the field of battle may convey an unfair advantage analogous to that which can occur in a business setting. Porter's Five Forces analysis provides the business equivalent of finding an adequate hill from which to fight. A firm effectively "fights from a hill" when the ability to control costs and control pricing exists. When a business is positioned so that these conditions exist, it is easier to maintain a competitive advantage over competitors. The five forces that govern business positioning (i.e., "selecting the business equivalent of the field of battle") are:

1. Rivalry
2. Barriers to Entry
3. Supplier Power
4. Buyer Power
5. Threat of Substitutes

To illustrate the power of the five forces in identifying an ideal position from which to fight, consider a situation where a firm does not have many competitors. The rivalry within the industry is therefore low, and the company is able to maintain a desirable price level. Further, consider that few substitutes exist for the product, and the barriers to entry within the industry are high. Because the number of new industry players is few, and customers have few alternatives, the price level of the product or service may be maintained at a high level. As a result, the firm has a high degree of supplier power. Finally, when the firm can control the cost of inputs to the firm's products and services, the company is said to have high buyer power over suppliers.

Strengths and Vulnerabilities

Returning again to the analogy of wartime, another major analysis point would be to consider the strength of the fighting force versus that of the enemy. This includes the discipline, training, and equipping of the fighting forces. Further, the strategic and tactical perspective of the generals leading the battle plays a key role in strategic advantage. The supply lines supporting the fighting force are also worthy of analysis—both for the defending force and the analysis of the supply lines of the enemy. Troops must be fed and provided with supplies and ammunition. Once analysis is undertaken, a plan of battle may coalesce around an observed vulnerability presented by the enemy force. Further, the fighting force also seeks out areas within its own fighting force that must be reinforced prior to engagement with the enemy. The considerations undertaken in the context of the analysis of a wartime playing field apply similarly to businesses. A business does not fight the enemy (i.e., "the competing firm") directly, but instead seeks to undermine the opponent by better serving available customers. In the marketplace in which the business battle is carried out, the supply of materials to make products or create services as well as the delivery of goods and services are essential components of a business victory. The supply chain is therefore carefully studied in any strategic planning initiative. However, in the military context, the supply lines, the military personnel, and the application of force together form the operations and delivery of the battle to the enemy. In the business domain, the picture is more complicated and represented by the value chain.

Analysis and the Value Chain

While the supply chain for both the business environment and military forces is an essential component of strategy, it is but one part of the whole of the firm. The totality of the firm may be described by the value chain.

The value chain is a framework used to understand all of the activities of the firm and how such activities result in earning profits. In the same way that project management provides structure to the process of strategic planning, the value chain offers a mechanism for systematically analyzing each component of the business (Figure 10).

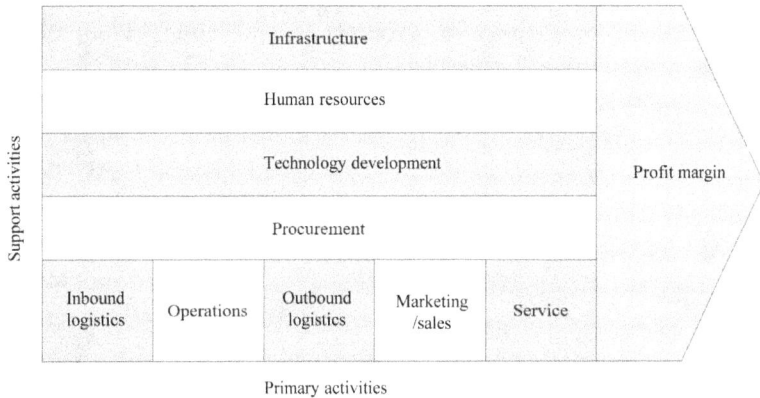

Figure 10 *The value chain*

The rationale behind the value chain is that everything that a firm produces must be something that some customer somewhere is willing to pay for. The amount paid for a product must cover the cost of developing, manufacturing, and marketing the product. The price must also cover the cost of capital. But, could this be said about all elements of the value chain? Does each element of the value chain bring in return greater than its cost to operation? Questions to be posed in the analysis of value chain strategic analysis include:

1. Cost: Does the value chain element add value beyond its cost?
2. Effectiveness: Is the value chain element effective in its assigned role?
3. Advantage: Is the value chain element a source of competitive advantage?
4. Benchmark: Does the value chain element meet, exceed, or fall behind cost and advantage performance of equivalent competitor supply chain elements?
5. Distinction: Does the value chain element have latent properties that if enhanced could have potential to develop or strengthen competitive advantage? Or, should the value chain element be considered as a candidate for outsourcing?

Using these questions as the basis for a strategic analysis of the value chain could be complemented with a relative scoring method. Using this method, the strategic analysis project could plot results for each value chain element using radar charts for an at-a-glance strategic profile. High scores would indicate strengths that could be a source of competitive advantage. Low scores, on the other hand, would suggest vulnerabilities, areas in need of additional resources, or candidates for partnership, merger, or acquisition (Figure 11).

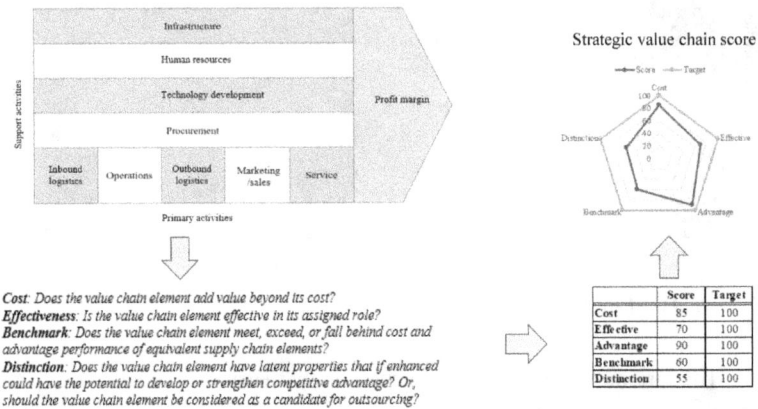

Cost: Does the value chain element add value beyond its cost?
Effectiveness: Is the value chain element effective in its assigned role?
Benchmark: Does the value chain element meet, exceed, or fall behind cost and advantage performance of equivalent supply chain elements?
Distinction: Does the value chain element have latent properties that if enhanced could have the potential to develop or strengthen competitive advantage? Or, should the value chain element be considered as a candidate for outsourcing?

	Score	Target
Cost	85	100
Effective	70	100
Advantage	90	100
Benchmark	60	100
Distinction	55	100

Figure 11 Strategic value chain analysis

Examples of Value Chain Competitiveness

When carrying out value chain strategic analysis, it is easier to keep a goal-oriented focus on developing an unfair strategic advantage by considering companies who employ specific elements of the value chain as their primary means of competing. Some notable examples include:

Inbound/Outbound Logistics: Walmart has long been known as a leader in the efficiency of its supply chain. The virtuous cycle employed by Walmart increases volume by reducing price, which in turn increases volume. High volumes spur supply chain efficiency thereby leading to reduced costs and lower prices—leading once again to higher volumes. The power of the Walmart supply chain has made it difficult for competitors to overtake. However, in recent years, Amazon's investment in inbound and outbound logistics has cut into Walmart's competitiveness. Further, Amazon's efficiency and its near-total focus on low prices and minimal brick-and-mortar locations may have led the market to tilt in favor of Amazon. When considering inbound and outbound logistics, these companies are exemplars. Analysis of this element of the company value chain would have a clear benchmark for sizing up existing competitiveness.

Marketing and Sales: Companies known for having a strong brand and that consistently rank high in annual sales are candidates for benchmarking in strategic supply chain analysis. Obvious candidates are those standout brands that have become the "go-to" option in its category—for example, Coca-Cola products, Dell computers, Target retail operations, and Microsoft for operating systems, cloud operations, and applications. The question to ask when evaluating this element of the supply chain is, "How does this company compare with the known market leaders in marketing and sales?" This question provides more effective answers when the question is narrowed down to leaders within the specific market that the company under analysis inhabits. On the other hand, the existing capabilities may be easily benchmarked against generic sales and marketing best practices of market leaders.

Service: Could the strategy of the company use exceptional service as its anchor? Whether or not this is a possibility depends on how the company under analysis compares with market leaders who differentiate themselves by means of service. Companies well known for service include names such as Chick-fil-A, Apple, and Trader Joe's. Could service be a source of competitive advantage if it currently is not? The good news for a company that may wish to employ service as a competitive differentiator is that it is an aspect of a company offering that may require only a change in culture rather than retooling and significant capital investment. The bad news is that some companies are better at changing culture than others. However, optimizing a firm using the project-led strategic planning and management technique will likely require changes in culture regardless of the specific source of competitive advantage adopted.

Technology Development: Technology expertise, including hardware, software, and intellectual property, is something that not all companies have at their disposal. Those who do not have it but aspire to use it as a source of competitive advantage may invest in technology development, acquire it, or merge with a company that does have it. Companies known to hold extensive technology portfolios include Samsung, Google, Apple, Microsoft, and Intel, to name a few. Unlike other elements of the supply chain, the analysis of technology as a competitive advantage could take a different direction. For example, an initial question might be "What latent technologies do we have that we could exploit in a way that we are not currently doing that would result in significant differentiation?" It is said that Intel asked questions such as these in its early days when making the decision to exit the memory business and exploit the new frontier of the microprocessor. A second question to consider relates to intellectual property. If a company makes the decision to further develop and exploit a latent technology, to what extent will this infringe upon companies who already hold extensive intellectual property portfolios?

It is observed that there are many elements in the company value chain, and for every element, there is likely to be an exemplar to consider. If the company could envision itself "stepping up" to deliver superior value chain elements consistent with identified benchmark candidates, then the possibility of using this value chain element as a source of competitive advantage exists. Otherwise, it may be a more prudent strategy to identify a different source of advantage and possibly de-emphasize or outsource the value chain component that is not capable of meeting or exceeding the results of industry exemplars.

SWOT Analysis

The value chain analysis will naturally reveal components of the business that strongly contribute to competitive advantage. Analysis of the value chain may also reveal components that detract from the overall success of the firm—or at least do not contribute to the same degree as the most successful value chain elements. Such analysis will naturally lead to the observation that "a chain is only as strong as its weakest link." The observation is therefore followed by a further analysis of each value chain component in detail. This examination of possible options and obvious or latent weaknesses is undertaken in a structured manner in strategic management by employing the SWOT analysis. It is the Strengths, Weaknesses, Opportunities, and Threats of the many components of the firm and its macroenvironment that are considered in strategic analysis, and each of these elements require the collection and analysis of data. In the business environment, there are additional intangibles that are considered in a holistic evaluation of the current situation. Intangibles include the regulatory or political environment, the economic and social environment that is likely to exist within the midterm time frame, and, finally, the technological context. A suggested mnemonic device for remembering the analysis components—Strengths, Weaknesses, Opportunities, Threats—and Political, Economic, Social, and Technological environment is succinctly stated in the phrase "SWOT the PEST."

SWOT Plus

One critique of the SWOT analysis is that it is descriptive rather prescriptive. SWOT identifies what is going well and what is not, but it says little about what should be done about perceived vulnerabilities—and why. One way to improve upon SWOT is to supplement it with goal- and action-oriented thinking. One way to do this is to use achieve/defend analysis. This works by asking the following questions:

1. In light of the observed strengths and weaknesses, what positions do we need to defend in the marketplace?
2. In light of the observed opportunities and threats, what positions do we need to achieve in the marketplace?

The addition of "achieve/defend" analysis takes the description of the internal and external environment and turns it into action-oriented results. The achieve/defend points that emerge from SWOT + will play a role in strategy formulation and choice. Clear calls for action will necessarily need to be aligned with the choice of strategy as well as the strategic implementation plan (Figure 12).

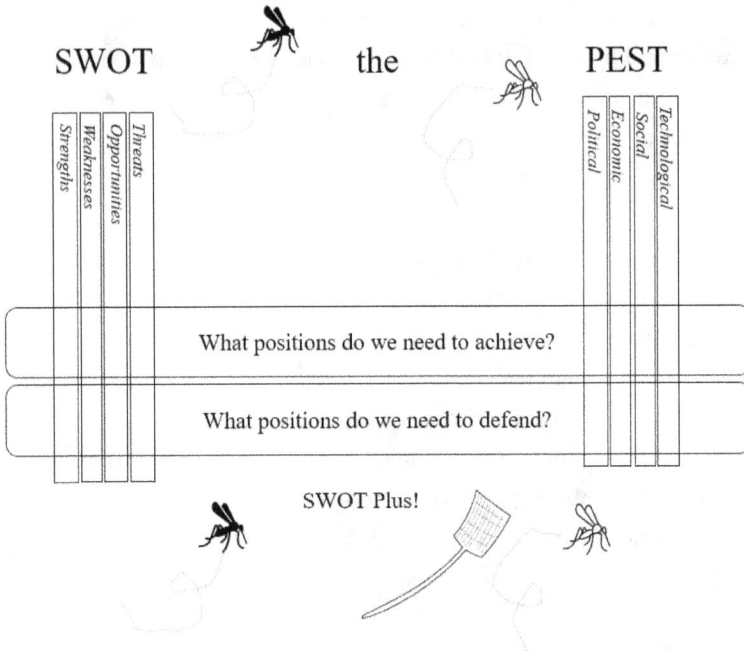

Figure 12 SWOT and SWOT Plus

Where Is the Project in Strategic Analysis?

When project management practice is married to the analysis process within strategic management, the effort is first chartered, the tangible deliverables are outlined with specificity in the project scope, and the activities that are required to produce the deliverables are identified, scheduled, and resourced. Analysis in strategic management is therefore initiated, planned, executed, monitored and controlled, and closed. The tangible and specific deliverables of the strategic analysis project are fed to the next strategic management phase of strategy formulation. It is project management process and practice that steers the effort of strategic analysis to produce specific and tangible deliverables. The tangible deliverable outputs of the strategic analysis project ultimately lead to "finding that hill from which to fight," or stated alternatively, "identifying the optimal industry position from which to do business," or in simple terms, "to identify a potential for an unfair advantage." What then are the deliverables of the strategic analysis project? The outputs of the process include defined reports and briefings that senior executives may use as the input to the strategy formulation project. It should be noted that the output of this process is distilled data rather than raw information. The work of collecting, sorting, distilling, analyzing, and finding hidden patterns in the collected data is the primary work of the project

CHAPTER 2

Components of the Analysis Process

The term "analysis" evokes the image of the expert sitting at a desk with pencil and paper making calculations. This image could apply to some aspects of strategic analysis. In reality, however, in the context of strategy development, the term "analysis" is not really one thing—but many things. Analysis is a construct consisting of multiple steps—many of which are sufficiently substantial that they may be managed as subprojects. Chapter 2 introduces the components of the process of strategic analysis.

A business succeeds or fails depending upon its strategic direction. Since this significant undertaking begins with an analysis of strategic position and internal competitiveness, it is important to be successful in the analysis process. A failure at this point could lead the company to move rapidly toward the wrong target. To mitigate this possibility, it makes sense to closely manage the effort by breaking down strategic analysis into its component parts beginning with data collection and ending with the reporting of the result. Each phase in the process may be chartered and managed as a project. Therefore, not only is strategic planning broken down into analysis, formulation, choice, and implementation, but each phase is further broken down into subprojects. In analysis, the underlying subprojects include data collection, analysis, and reporting (Figure 13).

The Data Collection Subproject

It is not unusual for the collection of data to proceed in an ad hoc manner. Often the data that is collected is the data that already exists within accounting and other enterprise systems. This data is likely to include sales, overhead costs, cost of goods sold (COGS), and customer activity.

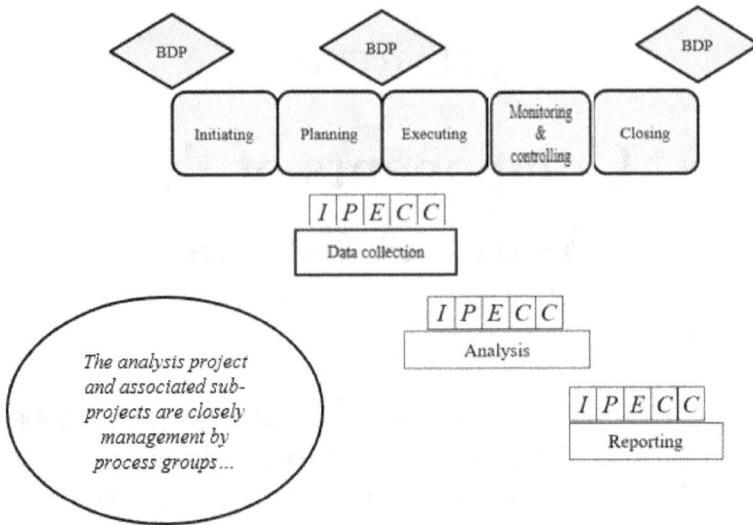

Figure 13 Strategic analysis project and subprojects

The process of chartering a project to collect data focuses the effort. Prior to the issuing of the project charter, the stakeholders involved in and surrounding the project are identified. Senior managers have a vested interest in the successful development of strategy, and it is from this group of stakeholders that the project team is usually selected. Company employees, vendors, the investor community, and clients and even competitors are all stakeholders to be identified, analyzed, and ranked in terms of importance. One of the purposes of stakeholder identification is to consider how the project will communicate to and engage with those identified. In strategic management projects, however, a certain amount of secrecy may be required. The stakeholder identification and analysis in strategy-related projects nearly turns project management practice "upside down" in some ways. This is because data collected and processed in strategic planning projects may be withheld from various stakeholder groups. Instead of determining with whom to communicate, stakeholder analysis may help determine with whom not to communicate. Why? Major strategic shifts, new organizations, or new products all involve highly sensitive and confidential information. Such information may initially only be communicated with those directly involved with strategic formulation or implementation who therefore have a need to know.

Chartering the Data Collection Subproject

The charter is a key part of initiating a project. In an organization that uses project management, the authority behind the charter of strategic planning projects emanates from the executive levels of the company. A cross-functional team of executives typically form a committee for the purpose of overseeing strategic planning projects. The executive team will be aware of who the appropriate resources are for completing the data collection work and will include such key names in the project charter.

The project charter authorizes a small project team to collect data and includes a simple statement of scope and objectives that the team is expected to complete. The charter also can serve as a reminder of the purpose that the collection of data is intended to serve. One way to do this is to direct the project to identify data sources and collect data that will allow the executive team to answer the following questions:

Is the company succeeding in its mission?
Is the company growing or declining?
Is revenue growing, declining, or stagnant?
Is profitability growing, declining, or stagnant?
Is company COGS and overhead cost in line with competitors?
What threats are on the horizon and where do they originate?
What vulnerabilities exist and what threats does the company face?
What should the company emphasize more? Deemphasize?
What latent opportunities should the company consider capitalizing on?
What positions does the company need to achieve? To defend?

The charter also succinctly outlines what data is to be collected, in what form it is to be delivered, and when the data will be presented for analysis. In addition, the charter includes schedule and budget constraints on the production of the data deliverables. It is expected that the project team will proceed to produce the required deliverables within the identified constraints and not reappear before the sponsoring executive committee until the deliverables are completed or the team determines that it will need to deviate in some way from the given constraints. To keep the project on track, it is recommended that the questions do not exceed five to ten so that the team avoids becoming defocused. Also, since each strategic question requires a specific data deliverable, it is possible to organize a work break-down structure (WBS) around each of the questions to be answered. Since the WBS is a structured outline of project deliverables, the deliverables will be data that could be used to answer the strategic questions. It is likely that each question will involve multiple data sources and result in different categories of data, including both quantitative and qualitative data. Because of the variety of activities involved, the data collection deliverables associated with each strategic question could be organized around work packages. Each work package includes the activities required to identify and collect data linked to the target question, the resource assignments, budget, and schedule estimate. Finally, the WBS deliverable will specify both the format of the data and the work package will spell out how the data is to be delivered as well as the associated acceptance criteria (Figure 14).

While the initial data collection project is small in scope, it still follows project management practice by chartering the project and developing the scope, schedule, and budget. The complete plan for the relatively small-scale data collection project, including all 10 knowledge areas, is still warranted albeit in abbreviated form. For example, the quality of the deliverables will require specification. Additionally, some external services or

Chartering the Data Collection Sub Project

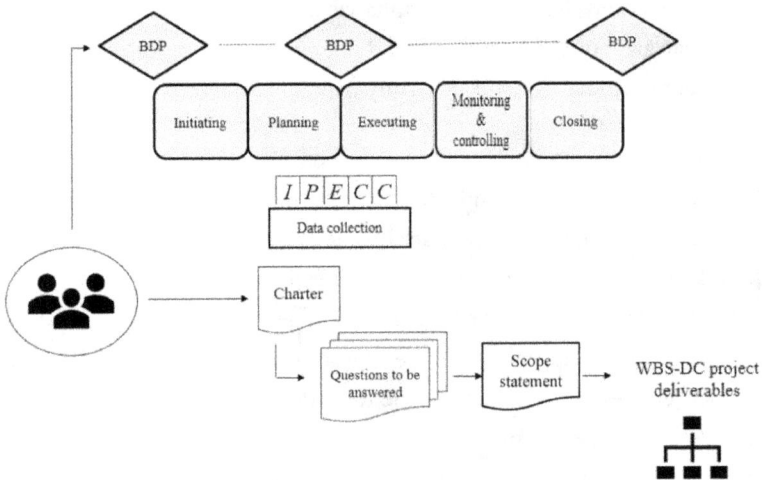

Figure 14 Chartering the data collection subproject

purchased data may be required resulting in an in-depth procurement plan. Each knowledge area scales as needed according to the depth of planning required for each deliverable. While the development of such plans does include some management overhead, the close management of the deliverables would appear warranted given the importance of the strategic planning effort. The structured approach created by managing data collection as a project ensures that the deliverables are produced, they are delivered in a timely manner, and, finally, they are created efficiently yet with the close oversight of senior management. This is superior to an ad hoc arrangement in the context of an unclear annual strategic management calendar accompanied by ambiguous requirements and deliverables.

The Data Analysis Subproject

The end of the data collection project triggers the next phase in the strategic planning cycle. This step is the chartering of the analysis project. The goal of this project is to take the data collected in the data collection project and perform work on the data with the goal of answering each of the strategic research questions. The questions link directly to data sources, categories of analysis, and results as indicated in Table 1.

The analysis project is chartered to produce specified analysis reports derived from the sources of data compiled in the data collection project. Analysis requires more work, resources, and tools. Further, analysis is likely to require multiple brainstorming meetings, discussion, debate, and critique of interim results. At the same time, analysis could continue unabated unless constrained by schedule and budget. The charter for the analysis effort includes the resources assigned to the core project team, the authorization to acquire additional resources as required (budget permitting), and also, describes the inputs data to the project as well as the exit criteria used to evaluate the result for successful completion.

The Reporting Subproject

Depending upon the size of the company, the ownership profile (public versus private), and, finally, the scale of the stakeholder community, the reporting of analysis results could be chartered as its own project just

Table 1 Sources, analysis, and results

Question	Data Sources	Analysis	Results
Is the company succeeding in its mission?	Client feedback	KPI analysis	Report
Is the company growing or declining?	Quarterly reports Annual reports	Financial metrics analysis	Spreadsheet, presentation
Is revenue growing, declining, or stagnant?	Quarterly reports Annual reports	Financial metrics analysis	Spreadsheet, presentation
Is profitability growing, declining, or stagnant?	Quarterly reports Annual reports	Financial metrics analysis	Spreadsheet, presentation
Is company COGS and overhead in line with competitors?	Quarterly reports Annual reports Benchmarking data	Financial metrics analysis, benchmark analysis	Spreadsheet, presentation
What threats are on the horizon and where do they originate?	Economic reports Industry reports Competitor studies	Risk analysis, forecasting	White paper
What vulnerabilities exist and what threats does the company face?	Economic reports Industry reports Competitor studies Internal documentation	Risk analysis	Spreadsheet, presentation
What should the company emphasize more? Deemphasize?	Economic reports Industry reports Competitor studies Internal documentation	SWOT analysis	Whitepaper, presentation
What latent opportunities should the company consider capitalizing on?	Economic reports Industry reports Competitor studies Internal documentation	SWOT + analysis	Whitepaper, presentation
What positions does the company need to achieve? To defend?	Economic reports Industry reports Competitor studies Internal documentation	SWOT + analysis	Whitepaper, presentation

as other preceding phases. An alternative to this approach is to manage the reporting of results as an extended communication and stakeholder engagement plan associated with the analysis project. The communication plan outlines who requires information, when, where, in what form, and how often. Further, the stakeholder management plan outlines which recipients of information have the greatest interest in the results of the strategic analysis, which have the greatest power to impact the analysis or make use of it, and, finally, what the nature of the interaction between the project team and stakeholders should be. Regardless of the approach taken, the results of the analysis of the strategic data are presented and then taken as input to the next steps of the strategic management process.

Changing the Subject

Things change in projects, and change is also to be expected in the context of strategic management projects. Consider, for example, the change to the strategic environment upon the launch of the first iPhone from Apple. This product transformed the industry from a landscape of flip style and "candy bar"–shaped phones designed primarily for voice communications and basic snapshots to a product with a touchscreen without physical buttons that was capable of Internet Web browsing. Imagine a cellphone company employing a project-led strategic management (PLSM) process in the midst of a significant industry disruption. A company could conceivably have analysis completed and have produced a detailed report of findings. What then? This is a matter of project governance.

CHAPTER 3

Governance in Strategic Projects

One of the most important duties of executive management is to determine the direction of the company. This is captured in the saying, "Leaders do the right thing, while managers do things right." While leaders hold the responsibility for strategy, it is not necessary nor practical for leadership to carry out all activities necessitated by the strategic management process. Much of the work is delegated to project teams. How do leaders ensure that project teams carry out strategic management duties consistent with the requirements of company leadership? This is implemented by means of the controlled delegation made possible by governance of the process. The governance of project-led strategic management is described in Chapter 3.

"Governance" is a big word that refers to some simple principles. The first principle is that projects are intentional exercises sanctioned at the top level of the company and implemented for the purpose of advancing the interests and strategic goals of the firm. The second principle is that the authorization that cascades down from senior management is bound by constraints. For example, the project charter outlines the constraints within which a project must live. Constraints include at minimum the triple constraint of scope, schedule, and budget. When the "subject is changed" at the strategic level of the macroenvironment, chances are that a major constraint must be violated. Typical project governance policy charters the project and gives the project team free rein to do what is necessary and without additional reporting or authorization until the next milestone in the project identified in the charter. There is one caveat—that is, the project team must appear before the project governing body and request reauthorization in the event that a constraint within the charter has been violated. In essence, the governing body views the project team in a manner similar to an external vendor and the charter is in effect a contract. A constraint violation is therefore a contract violation, and the project team therefore must either request a revised contract or the contract is terminated. Returning to the example of the iPhone disruption of the smartphone industry, the project governance mechanism is capable of readily handling such a major disruption of the strategic planning process. In fact, it may be argued that breaking the process into a series of discrete projects better supports interruption and redirection than an ongoing operation that performs strategic activities on a continuous basis. Change is governed by process, and the process may be stopped or started as needed.

Strategy and Integrated Change Control

It is also possible, and likely probable, that the process of discovery within all phases of strategic project management will lead to new information, new challenges, or, as previously mentioned, sources of disruption that could be managed using existing change control processes outlined in the PMBOK. Any stakeholder encountering an issue affecting the baseline scope, schedule, or budget may seek change by submitting a change request to the CCB or "Change Control Board." Given the strategic nature of the projects involved in this work, it is likely that the CCB members will include members of the governing executive panel—or may in fact be the governing body itself. The important conclusion that arises from the evaluation of how change is incorporated within the project-led strategy process is that the apparent high-structured sequence of projects chartered to develop and implement strategy does not impede the need for change. In fact, change is welcomed, and it fits naturally within project management methodology (Figure 15).

Governance and Executive Ownership

Governance is observed to offer a clean mechanism for delegating the work while retaining tight control and oversight. The contractual relationship created by the charter and the budget, schedule, and scope

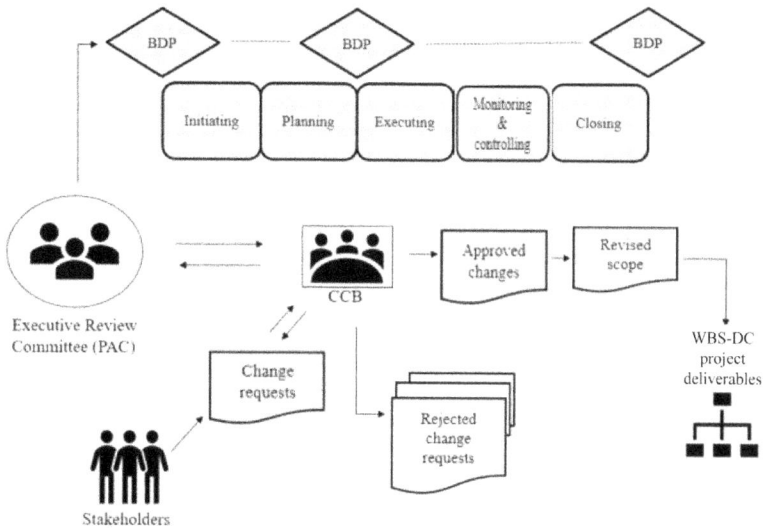

Figure 15 **Integrated change control**

constraints places clear boundaries on what the project team may and may not do. In the same way as a contractual relationship with an outside partner or vendor, the terms of the contract may not be violated unless all parties agree to do so. This directive is written into the charter so that the executive team need not expend time and energy tracking every move of the project teams assigned to carry out the chartered mission. This method of oversight—"'hands off' control until it needs to be 'hands on'"—is carried forward throughout all phases of strategic management including the implementation of strategy. Additionally, the governance process adds value by virtue of incorporating a cross-functional executive team into strategic management oversight, thereby leading to the potential of a more holistic view in decision making as well as the possibility of triggering new ideas and insights. A visionary leader may carry the day when it comes to pursuing a specific strategic initiative, but the vision is also tempered by the input of the empowered executive governance team. This is useful for those cases when the visionary leader "gets it wrong." Further, the workings of an effective governance team may spur the development of ideas when a less visionary and more operationally focused leader is at the helm.

CHAPTER 4

Strategy Formulation

Strategic analysis develops the inputs to the strategic formulation process. Using the analogy of cooking, strategic analysis provides the ingredients. Once the ingredients have been collected, it is now time to decide exactly "what kind of cake ought to be baked." Or, more accurately, the formulation process answers the question of "What exactly should we bake?" The process of making the decision of what to bake, or what form the strategy will ultimately take, occurs within the strategy formulation process. This is described in Chapter 4.

The term "formulation" in the strategic planning process implies development or design. An analogy could be made to the development of a blueprint. In the case of company strategy, however, the formulation of strategy involves evaluating several strategic possibilities resulting from analysis of the internal and external environment. In project management terms, the formulation of strategy constitutes the development of proposals. For example, the analysis in strategic planning identifies opportunities available in the macroenvironment that matches company capabilities. The senior executive, by means of project management, would charter one or more projects to prepare plans for implementation. The completed proposals are then weighed according to strategic criteria such risk, firm capabilities, and potential for return. The output of the strategic formulation process becomes the input to strategic choice.

It is observed that the project management process framework organizes project management work in terms of inputs, tools and techniques, and outputs. Further, the output of one process becomes the input to another. Likewise, the output of the analysis phase of strategic planning becomes the input to the formulation phase. The project team chartered to formulate strategy uses the deliverables from the strategic analysis project (or projects), and then uses the information to develop strategic options with the goal in mind of delivering a few select strategic plan candidates as outputs. These deliverables feed into the strategic choice phase. In summary, therefore, the formulation or development of the strategy involves a consideration of possibilities that are likely to result in successful positioning and successful outcomes. Which option is likely to deliver optimal results? This is a decision reserved for the strategic choice phase.

Formulation as the Feasibility Subproject

Formulation of strategy involves not only what *should* be done to attain a competitive advantage, but also what *can* be done. To provide an analogy in the world of sports, all sports teams should aspire to become champions—be it the World Cup, the World Series, or the Super Bowl. However, it is also true that not all sports teams are capable of achieving this. A component of strategy formulation must therefore involve a measure of feasibility analysis. A feasibility analysis requires the systematic consideration and answering of the following questions:

1. Do we have the know-how to carry out such a strategy?
2. Do we have the required technology?
3. Do we have adequate funding to execute the strategy?
4. Do we have the human resources required to implement the strategy?
5. Will this strategy create an unfair advantage for the company?
6. Is this strategy something that we could carry out better than competitors?

It is observed that strategy formulation therefore requires serious answers to the "Can we do it?" and "Should we do it?" questions (Figure 16).

Formulation as Alignment Subproject

Strategic possibilities are reveal when the firm considers strategic positioning, generic strategies, and unique strategic capabilities. There are other less tangible factors to be considered, and this involves the culture or style of doing business. Strategic options are said to be in alignment

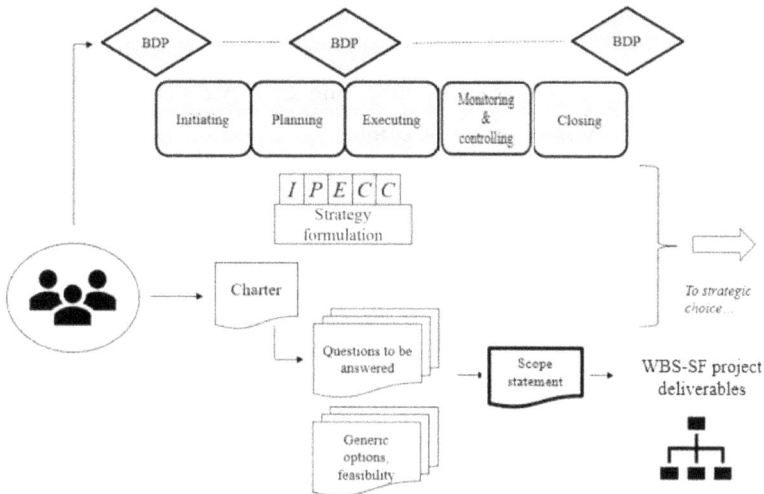

Figure 16 The formulation project

with the culture and mindset of the firm when they are consistent with the firm's traditional way of doing things. Said in another way, a strategic option aligns well with a company if the activities required to implement the strategy are observed to be consistent with its natural way of doing business. As an example, consider a company that has traditionally thrived as a developer and manufacturer of products. Such a company is familiar with analyzing client requirements, converting these into specifications, creating a product plan, chartering a development project, and, finally, transferring the result to manufacturing so that sales may commence. If a proposed new strategy was outside of the bounds of this type of familiar business process, such as the development of a service or the creation of a software application, the strategy would not likely align well with the company culture. This does not mean that the proposed strategy would fail, but it would mean that its implementation would be more challenging.

Alignment and Systems Thinking

Systems thinking provides a lens for how an organization truly works in practice. Rather than being a static structure, the organization is composed of a dynamic set of interconnected linkages. When things go wrong in the development and implementation of policy, often it is because the senior management fails to adequately understand how the "puzzle pieces" of the organization fit together. This is why the "law of unintended consequences" applies in policy and strategy development. Management has a vision of where the company needs to go and what it needs to do, but since the organization and the cause and effect linkages are not fully grasped, the organization fails to achieve the goal. Instead, different outcomes and problems emerge and few are able to understand why. Formulating a strategy that aligns with the underlying mechanism of the "system" and "interconnected linkages" within the firm presumes that strategy developers understand it. It pays then during strategy formulation to ensure that the system is understood prior to formulating a strategy that aligns with it.

Alignment and the McKinsey 7S

The McKinsey 7S framework illustrates how elements of the firm interlock. This framework does bear a relationship to systems thinking as it portrays an organization as a system. It goes beyond the principle of systems thinking, however, by defining seven key conceptual elements of the firm as well as explaining how they relate to each other. The seven elements include three elements referred to as "hard" (Strategy, Structure, and Systems) as well as four elements considered as "soft" (Shared Values, Skills, Style, and Staff). The question to ask in the formulation of strategy is, "To what extent does the proposed strategy align with the hard and soft elements of the firm?" Also, "In what way would the elements need to change in order to adopt the new strategy?" A strategy with maximum impact to the elements of the 7S framework may be one that is unlikely to align well with the company's way of doing things. This is especially true of the four "soft" elements of Shared Values, Skills, Style, and Staff. What is in question in strategy formulation is the hard three of Strategy, Structure, and Systems. A test of alignment could involve testing the impact of proposed changes to the hard three as it relates to the soft four. A possible assessment of alignment among key stakeholders could be carried out using a series of questions using a simple survey instrument. When such an instrument is employed, each key stakeholder is presented with a slide deck of various strategic options deemed to be a reasonable fit with the reports emerging from the analysis project. Upon reviewing each strategic option, stakeholders respond to the accompanying short survey.

The 7S Strategy Formulation Alignment Survey

For each statement, record your level of agreement for the purposes of strategy formulation:

1. The proposed change in *strategy* is a significant departure from the shared values of the company.
   a. Strongly agree
   b. Agree
   c. Neither agree nor disagree
   d. Disagree
   e. Strongly disagree
2. The proposed change in *strategy* requires skill sets that differ from our current skill profile.
   a. Strongly agree
   b. Agree
   c. Neither agree nor disagree
   d. Disagree
   e. Strongly disagree
3. The proposed change in *strategy* requires a significant change in our style of doing business.
   a. Strongly agree
   b. Agree
   c. Neither agree nor disagree
   d. Disagree
   e. Strongly disagree
4. The proposed change in *strategy* requires a significant change in our staffing profile.
   a. Strongly agree
   b. Agree
   c. Neither agree nor disagree
   d. Disagree
   e. Strongly disagree

5. The proposed change in *structure* is a significant departure from the shared values of the company.
   a. Strongly agree
   b. Agree
   c. Neither agree nor disagree
   d. Disagree
   e. Strongly disagree

6. The proposed change in *structure* requires skill sets that differ from our current skill profile.
   a. Strongly agree
   b. Agree
   c. Neither agree nor disagree
   d. Strongly disagree
   e. Disagree

7. The proposed change in *structure* requires a significant change in our style of doing business.
   a. Strongly agree
   b. Agree
   c. Neither agree nor disagree
   d. Disagree
   e. Strongly disagree

8. The proposed change in *structure* requires a significant change in our staffing profile.
   a. Strongly agree
   b. Agree
   c. Neither agree nor disagree
   d. Disagree
   e. Strongly disagree

9. The proposed change in *staff* will significantly impact the culture of the company.
   a. Strongly agree
   b. Agree
   c. Neither agree nor disagree
   d. Disagree
   e. Strongly disagree

10. The proposed change in *staff* will significantly impact the enterprise environmental factors of the company.
    a. Strongly agree
    b. Agree
    c. Neither agree nor disagree
    d. Disagree
    e. Strongly disagree

When responses are coded from 1 to 5 (1 = strongly agree), a score less than 3 is generally indicative of a weak alignment of the proposed strategy with the firm.

Alignment and the Balanced Scorecard

Systems thinking has as its emphasis the underlying, and often hidden, connections between the subsystems of the firm, while the 7S framework implicitly acknowledges systems thinking with its attempts to model the firm with a specific set of hard and soft components. The balanced scorecard in similar fashion identifies elements of the firm that are considered important for its successful management. Unlike the McKinsey 7S framework, the balanced scorecard identifies four categories for which the leadership must devote attention. The categories include the customer perspective, financial perspective, internal processes, and innovation. These four categories are often displayed as a wheel that revolves around the central core of vision and strategy. The linkages between the four categories on the balanced scorecard "wheel" and the interior strategic "hub" suggest that when the strategy changes, there are implications for the management of the firm. Therefore, replacing the strategy and vision of the company likely necessitates a review of customers, financials, internal processes, and sources of innovation. Like the 7S and systems thinking paradigm, proposed strategic changes that more closely fit the existing "wheel" of the scorecard could be said to be in alignment. Further, alignment suggests the enhanced possibility of successful implementation and change. Using the same methodology as the 7S model alignment assessment, the strategic alignment of potential strategies from the perspective may be assessed by means of a survey instrument (Figure 17).

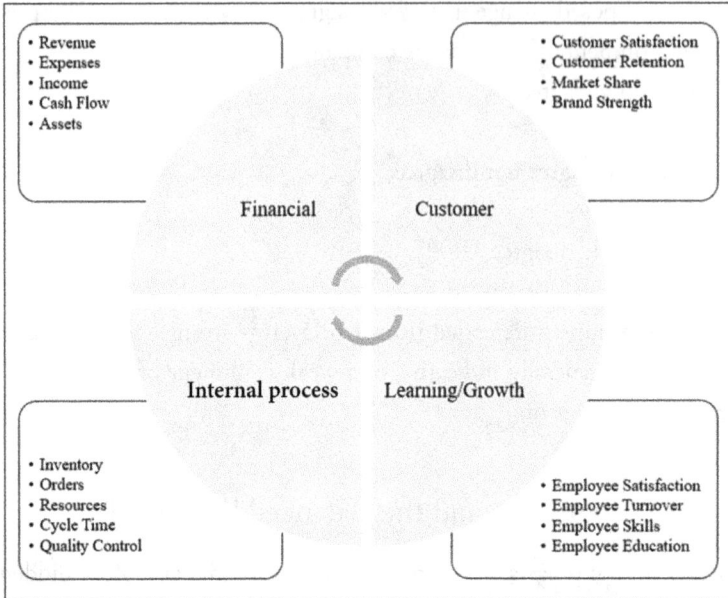

Figure 17 The balanced scorecard

The Balanced Scorecard Strategy Formulation Alignment Survey

For each statement, record your level of agreement for the purposes of strategy formulation:

1. The proposed change in *strategy* is likely to have a significant negative impact on the revenues of the firm.
   a. Strongly agree
   b. Agree
   c. Neither agree nor disagree
   d. Disagree
   e. Strongly disagree
2. The proposed change in *strategy* is likely to have a significant negative impact on the fixed and variable costs of the firm.
   a. Strongly agree
   b. Agree
   c. Neither agree nor disagree
   d. Disagree
   e. Strongly disagree

3. The proposed change in *strategy* is likely to have a significant negative impact on the profitability of the firm.
   a. Strongly agree
   b. Agree
   c. Neither agree nor disagree
   d. Disagree
   e. Strongly disagree

4. The proposed change in *strategy* is likely to have a significant impact on the customers of the firm.
   a. Strongly agree
   b. Agree
   c. Neither agree nor disagree
   d. Disagree
   e. Strongly disagree

5. The proposed change in *strategy* is likely to require seeking out new customers and markets for the products and services of the firm.
   a. Strongly agree
   b. Agree
   c. Neither agree nor disagree
   d. Disagree
   e. Strongly disagree

6. The proposed change in *strategy* is likely to have a significant impact on employee turnover.
   a. Strongly agree
   b. Agree
   c. Neither agree nor disagree
   d. Disagree
   e. Strongly disagree

7. The proposed change in *strategy* is likely to require significant changes in internal business processes.
   a. Strongly agree
   b. Agree
   c. Neither agree nor disagree
   d. Disagree
   e. Strongly disagree

8. The proposed change in *strategy* is likely to impact the efficiency and productivity of the firm.
   a. Strongly agree
   b. Agree
   c. Neither agree nor disagree
   d. Disagree
   e. Strongly disagree

When responses are coded from 1 to 5 (1 = strongly agree), a score less than 3 is generally indicative of a weak alignment of the proposed strategy with the firm.

Alignment and PROSCI change management

The PROSCI change management model (from **Pro**fessional and **Sci**ence) is focused on awareness as well as readiness for change. Alignment in the case of the PROSCI method is more a matter of scoring the readiness of the organization and the individual. Finally, PROSCI seeks to clarify both the know-how of the individuals in the organization in terms of how prepared they are to carry out the change (Figure 18).

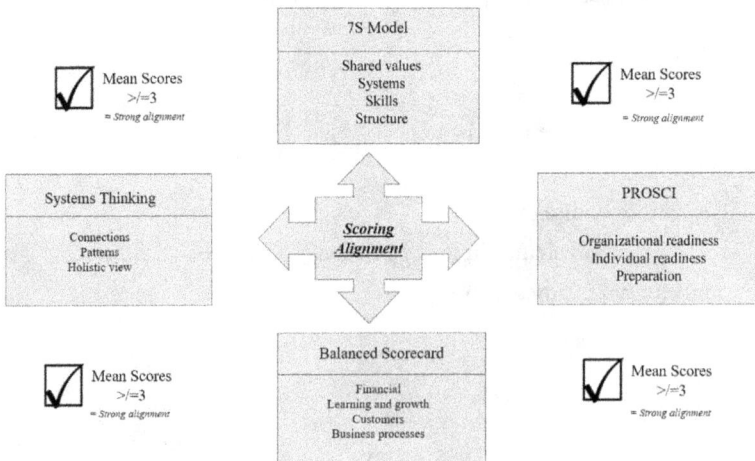

Figure 18 Alignment survey results

Outputs of Formulation

What specifically would a strategy formulation project deliver? In short, strategic formulation delivers strategic options that are likely to fit the structure, culture, and capability of the company. However, this question is answered first by examining the input to the project, which is the output of the analysis and reporting project. The analysis project reports the state of the strategic landscape as communicated by the study of the examination of industry structure in terms of Porter's forces. A further output of the analysis project is an in-depth evaluation of strengths, weaknesses, opportunities, and threats, possibly including benchmarking data from key competitors. What results is, in effect, a matrix of strategic indicators—some of which must be countered by the strategy of the firm and some which are opportunities for which the company will capitalize. The good news for the formulation project team is that industry examples coupled with academic analysis provide templates for strategy that may be adopted or modified as necessary to counter the challenges and capture the opportunities. Several prominent strategic templates are outlined and described in the following sections.

Porter's Generic Strategies

Porter offers insights on how to approach strategic positioning within the five forces. The generic approaches include cost, differentiation, and focus. A cost strategy is not the same as "pricing." Competing on cost means that the firm is able to operate at a cost less than all competitors. If a company offers lower prices than competitors without enjoying a beneficial cost advantage, then eventually the firm will be driven out of business. An advantageous cost position is created in many ways and may include specialized know-how, geographical location, or advanced technology. Porter further warns against attempting to use this approach by means of process improvement initiatives. If one company is able to implement improvements, another could be expected to respond in kind. Since competitive advantage is bestowed on a company by virtue of its inability to be duplicated, a simple operational approach to cost reduction is rarely considered to be a source of competitive advantage.

At the opposite end of the strategic spectrum lies the generic strategy of differentiation. Unlike the low-cost strategy, differentiation seeks an advantage due to offering "something special." A good way to visualize the difference is to compare a luxury good with a low-priced commodity. For example, the difference between a Rolex and a Timex watch is obvious. Timex does not attempt to be Rolex and vice versa. Porter cautions companies against attempting to mix the two generic strategies. Companies who attempt to "do a little of both" risk ending up "somewhere in the middle." This occurs when companies competing on cost begin to add features and options so as to differentiate from competitors. The resulting products are no longer lowest in cost, and at the same time, do not have sufficient appeal to compete with differentiated competitors. Likewise, a company competing with the generic strategy of differentiation that attempts to compete on cost may fall out of favor as a brand.

The degree of focus is the final element of generic strategy that is considered in the strategic formulation process. The idea behind focus relates to the scope of the market or markets targeted by the firm. For example, will the firm compete within a large market or will it focus on a niche? Firms are often tempted to target a very large market because the size suggests large revenues, and large revenues often suggest big profits. This is not always the case, however, as large markets tend to attract a large number of competitors. When competitors abound, the price level is often observed to erode, and profits decline. A wide focus may not necessarily pay, which is likely the source of the saying "niches have riches." Regardless of the choice of cost versus differentiation, focus is therefore an essential element for consideration in strategy formulation.

Resource-Based Strategy

Porter's view of strategy is related to positioning within industry, so that an "unfair" competitive advantage is developed. The idea implicit in this concept of strategy is that regardless of the capability of the company, a favorable position within the industry will lead to success. The resource-based view (or RBV) of strategy proposes that positioning can only go so far. It is the capabilities of the firm that are said to play the key role in the attainment of a sustained competitive advantage. When this view of strategy is taken into account, the resources of the firm are considered using the VRIO analysis. VRIO stands for Valuable, Rare, Inimitable, and Organization. Questions asked in RBV strategy formulation include:

1. Does our firm feature resources that are highly valued in the industry and markets in which we participate?
2. Do we have resources that are not typically found elsewhere?
3. Are competitors able to replicate the unique capabilities of the resources in the firm?
4. Are the resources of the firm organized in such a way that they produce effective results?

The resource-based view mirrors the view of the sports team building up resources for the purposes of dominating the field and winning championships. In sports, positioning is not a factor in season-to-season competition. Instead, the sustained competitive advantage comes through the superiority of the capabilities of the team members as well as how they are managed. This approach to management is therefore one that bears considering in the process of strategy formulation.

The "Blue Ocean"

There is a school of thought in strategy formulation that rejects the generic formulation of Porter. This approach suggests that rather than follow the rules of cost versus differentiation, embark on a path that ignores such rules. It does so by creating a new market. A new market has no existing competitors and therefore appears as a wide open "Blue Ocean" with unlimited possibilities. With no competitors and no previous history, a company opening a Blue Ocean creates the rules of the game. In such a scenario, a company may offer differentiated products and services combined with low cost—or other options. When a company creates its own rules, the strategic possibilities are endless. However, the challenge to this strategy is finding this unique angle that creates an innovative formulation of value that currently does not exist. In strategy formulation, this requires asking, "What can we do that creates our own unique market space where we can innovate and dominate the market in a novel way?" The Blue Ocean bears consideration in strategy formulation as it breaks the mold of convention. On the other hand, it is one of those great ideas that in practice is difficult to achieve. At minimum, a "How could we create our Blue Ocean?" brainstorming activity would be a reasonable option to employ in strategic formulation (Figure 19).

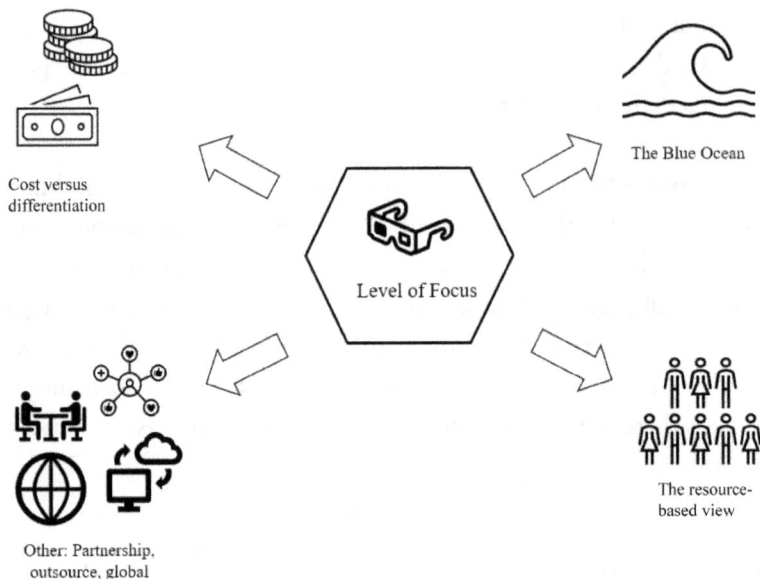

Figure 19 Strategic formulation options

CHAPTER 5

Strategic Choice

Strategy without analysis and strategy formulation lack foundation and substance and keep strategy from being nothing more than intuition and guesswork. However, there comes a time when the decision—the choice—of strategy must be made. Strategic choice is never easy, and this is why "analysis paralysis" often prevails. Fortunately, project management offers an array of tools for selecting between projects and deciding between which to do and not to do. These tools are a good fit for making strategic decisions and are introduced in Chapter 5.

The strategy formulation process produces a selection of possible strategic initiatives designed to lead to success in achieving an advantage over competitors. Some initiatives may be better than others. However, strategic management involves making choices, and the best options for execution may not be easily determined. This is a dilemma that has long existed in the context of project management. In addition to process guidance for planning and executing projects, project management practice also provides supporting processes for project selection. Choosing between possible projects to charter within the context of funding constraints therefore led to the evolution of valuable tools and techniques. The specific tangible goals of the strategic initiative along with its limited time span suggest that strategic initiatives are projects. Given that strategic initiatives are projects, project management practice therefore may also be employed in the context of strategic choice. Therefore, project selection tools may be applied to decisions associated with selecting strategic initiatives. Project management practice suggests that the determination of which projects will and will not be chartered is linked to the strategy of the firm. Since the strategy in this case is in the process of being developed, deciding which course of action will be taken assumes that the company clearly understands its mission and how strategic actions are linked to that mission. The decision-making tools offered by project management are designed to determine by qualitative, quantitative, or mixed methods, which project choices optimally align with strategic goals of the firm. Project management practice applied to choosing between project alternatives is therefore observed to be a set of business processes that have application in making strategic choices. Some methods include:

Strategic Checklist: A strategic checklist identifies those elements that if found to be in place within a strategic initiative make the strategy more attractive and in better alignment with the mission of the company. When strategic initiatives are compared, a project or initiative that "ticks more boxes" than another project will be more likely to be selected. The downside of using the checklist approach is the "ticking boxes" comes with the implicit assumption that all options are equally valid and important. This is not necessarily the case.

Weighted Ranking Tool: A weighted selection tool functions in the same manner as a checklist. However, unlike a checklist where all elements carry the same level of importance, a weighted ranking system allows managers the opportunity to recognize some elements of the list as being more important than others. The significance of each element is indicated by using weights, and then final scores are computed by multiplying scores by the weights of each strategic category. This method facilitates comparison of multiple proposals where the highest score is selected.

Quantitative Techniques: One of the most common quantitative tools to choose between projects is the decision tree. The decision tree provides managers to model probabilities and outcomes of different courses of action. Highly complex decision trees may be used to model multiple initiatives at the same time and to evaluate the interaction between the options as well as associated opportunity costs. When decision trees are employed, the outcome of possible strategies may be evaluated by assigning probabilities and payoffs of undertaking strategies in the context of various market conditions. A decision tree has limitations in that the limited number of branches can never reflect the totality of possibilities that may unfold within the macroenvironment. Further, the probabilities assigned for each branch are fixed—and there is no guarantee that the real-world outcomes will match assigned probabilities. Also, the probabilities assigned to elements of the decision tree are often nothing more than expert judgment or educated guesses. A way around this is to use probability distributions for each decision tree element rather than fixed probabilities. This supports the use of Monte Carlo analysis to model outcomes and to provide more substantial guidance associated with making a strategic decision and choosing a strategy. When using this approach, the decision tree may also be significantly expanded to incorporate a wide array of factors to create rich scenario possibilities. Decision tree templates are widely available for Microsoft Excel on the Web.

Financial Methods: Financial methods range from the simple to the complex. Some of the more rudimentary methods include the payback period and the ROI (return on investment). These simple calculations answer the questions, "When will we get our money back?" and "Will the money returned by the investment in this project be commensurate with the effort and risk undertaken?" The payback method and the ROI are considered simple because they typically do not necessarily consider the time value of money in the analysis. The payback period may be useful for a short term or midterm strategic time frame. Longer time periods are more challenging when employed in payback period analysis because longer time ranges introduce increasing uncertainty. For some strategic choices, it may be unclear whether the payback for money invested will ever occur. ROI by way of contrast simply divides the profit number by the total investment. This metric may be carried out at any time in the course of strategy implementation. Methods that take into account the time value of money (TVM) are observed to be stronger because such methods do a better job of taking uncertainty into consideration. This is because money in the bank today is worth more than the promise of money at a future date, so a more sophisticated analysis recognizes this fact. Selection methods that do take this into account include the Net Present Value (NPV) calculation as well as the IRR (Internal Rate of Return). The NPV answers the question, "Will this initiative return more, or less than if I simply put my money in the bank (or otherwise secure financial instrument)?" The IRR seeks the answer to the question, "What percentage of return will this initiative effectively produce?" Initiatives evaluated using these methods are ranked—with highest NPV and/or IRR numbers being preferred.

Each of the methods used for selecting strategic courses of action are the same as those provided in the PMBOK. This makes sense because a strategic proposal or initiative fits the definition of a project. Further, in the same way as a project, a strategic initiative is intended to produce benefits for the company. Such strategic benefits may be evaluated in the same way as the benefits resulting from project deliverables—hence—the same selection tools are employed (Figure 20).

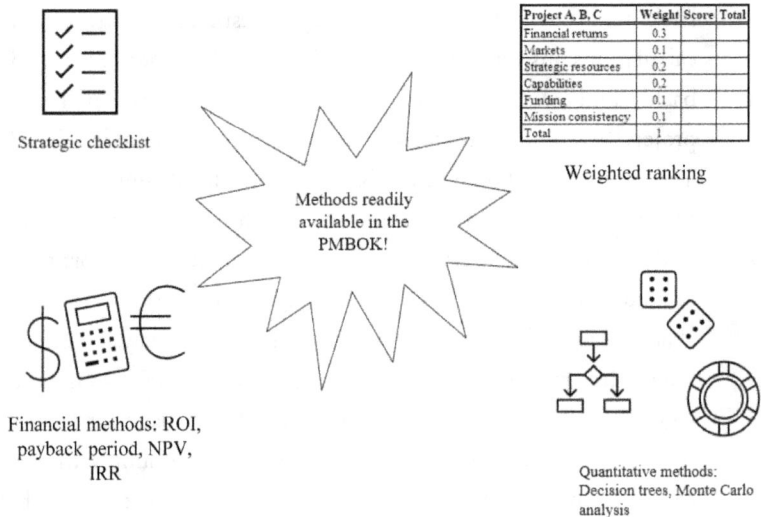

Strategic checklist

Project A, B, C	Weight	Score	Total
Financial returns	0.3		
Markets	0.1		
Strategic resources	0.2		
Capabilities	0.2		
Funding	0.1		
Mission consistency	0.1		
Total	1		

Weighted ranking

Methods readily available in the PMBOK!

Financial methods: ROI, payback period, NPV, IRR

Quantitative methods: Decision trees, Monte Carlo analysis

Figure 20 Strategic choice methods

Operational Decision-Making Tools

Pareto

Often a change in strategy is triggered when firms face an increasing number of challenges and barriers associated with fulfilling its mission. When it becomes clear that something is not working, it is time for a change. But what specifically needs to change? Often it is the case that the largest number of issues arises from a small subset of the organization. The Pareto rule supports this with the observation that 80 percent of the problems arise from 20 percent of the customers, products, or other unit of analysis. Perhaps the company is facing problems for which the current strategic profile is unable to overcome. On the other hand, it may be the case that a small number of factors are generating a large number of challenges. A Pareto analysis of issues encountered within the firm may focus the attention to strategic choices that impact most heavily on the small set of issues that act as barriers to success.

Root Cause

While Pareto analysis tends to narrow the focus on "what counts," root cause analysis takes such analysis a step further. Just when the analysis of ongoing problems in the firm appears to be narrowing down, this is not the time to end the exercise. If the root cause of poor competitiveness is not fully understood, any strategy applied to improve results will be misguided and will "solve the wrong problem." When "hot on the trail" of a strategic change that will address current weaknesses, it pays to think again and ask "why." Root Cause Analysis, or RCA, is often implemented using a fishbone diagram along with the "Five Whys" exercise. To give a simple example, consider the following strategic Five Whys exercise:

1. Why are sales down in the current fiscal year?
   a. The data suggests that customers are buying less product.
2. Why are customers buying less product?
   a. Survey data indicates that customers are instead buying the competitor's product.
3. Why are they buying the competitor's product?
   a. Market research data indicates that the competitor's product includes features missing in our product.
4. Why are features missing from our product?
   a. Analysis of the product requirements document indicates that the features of interest were missed in the product requirements.
5. Why were the requirements incomplete?
   a. Interview data from the product planning group suggests that the new product was an incremental development based on the previous generation product. Novel features were neglected in the development of the product specification.

As a result of the Five Whys and RCA, it becomes increasingly clear that the failure to compete in the current fiscal year is related to a problem in the requirements collection and analysis. When selecting a strategy, the ideal option would be one that plays a role in improving this issue.

Scatter Diagram

Firms today encounter an endless array of data from internal operations, transactions, and the macroenvironment. Often in this sea of data it is easy to lose track of important relationships. It is the scatter diagram that can aid in seeing patterns that are not otherwise obvious. For example, if the company is doing more of something—such as spending more on marketing—does the sales volume trend in the same direction? If it does not, what, if anything, does this suggest? An effective strategy is one that is grounded in reality. The best strategic choices are those that successfully capture the causal relationships between variables and act on them in such a way that the competitiveness of the firm is improved. It should be remembered though that "association is not causation." This means that an apparent relationship between variables may not be an actual relationship. Consider once again the link between marketing budget and sales volume. If both increase, was one actually the cause of the other? Possibly—but this is a relationship that requires confirmation. For example, it may be the case that a few key products were discounted during the same period thereby introducing an intervening variable that is the actual cause of the sales increase. Just as in the case of the Pareto analysis—once a solution appears to be in sight—in this case with an apparent relationship within a scatter diagram—it is time once again to ask, "Why?"

Control Chart

Strategies that produce outstanding results run the risk of falling short of expectations over time. A classic example is the sailing ship industry during the period when steamships began to take significant market share. The previously successful strategy of building sailing ships for speed—and rapid passage across the Atlantic—eventually broke down in the face of continued improvement of steam competition. The gradual decay of this business and the rapid rise of competition is something that could be tracked and monitored in a format very similar to a control chart. Once key business metrics such as sales volume, efficiency, and productivity begin to drift in a single direction over multiple accounting periods—strategic intervention is warranted. Another example of the use of the control chart is to monitor how well the strategy is tracking to the next strategic milestone or waypoint. There are times when the strategy can begin to drift off course. A control chart monitoring metrics associated with the existing strategy can signal possible strategic drift thereby leading to strategic intervention (Figure 21).

Operational strategic choice methods

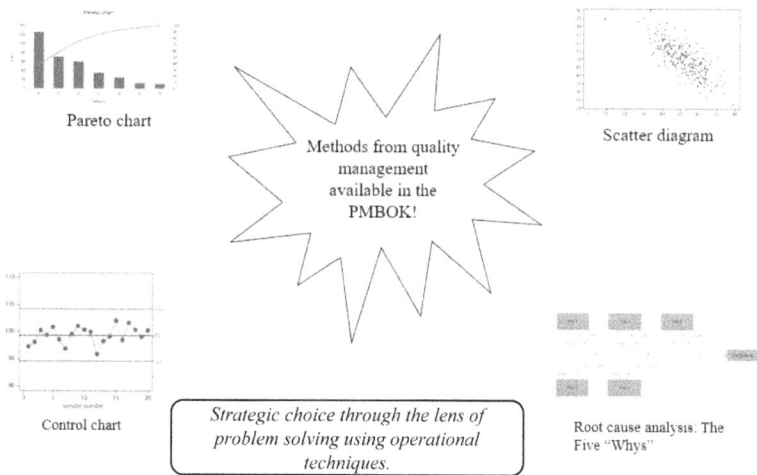

Pareto chart

Scatter diagram

Methods from quality management available in the PMBOK!

Control chart

Root cause analysis: The Five "Whys"

Strategic choice through the lens of problem solving using operational techniques.

Figure 21 Operational strategic choice problem solving

CHAPTER 6

Project Management in Strategy Implementation

Strategy implementation often requires new organizational structures, new hires, new processes, and the roll-out of new activities. Such initiatives differ from the day-to-day continuous operational activities. Since they are temporary and unique, strategic initiatives qualify as projects and may be managed as such. Doing so provides the process framework support as well as the close management required to see strategic initiatives through to a successful end. Chapter 6 explains how to implement strategy by managing strategic initiatives as projects.

It is observed that strategic analysis and strategy formulation process may be viewed as projects and formally chartered to produce both a strategic profile as well as plans for implementation. Further, strategic decision making may employ project selection tools. This operational concept brings the early phases of strategic management into clear focus and provides a framework for crisp, cross-functional execution along with the production of tangible outcomes. Although the application of project management at this strategic tier of the firm may appear novel, the idea of using project management to scope, plan, and execute strategic initiatives may not be. A strategic initiative is a temporary activity carried out to achieve or enable a strategic objective. For example, a strategic goal to increase sales by 10 percent may require a special effort to hire a specific number of salespeople to target new markets or customers (Figure 22).

This special hiring effort is a project and could be chartered as such and led by a project manager. This is but one example, however. The fundamentals of using project management in strategic implement involve the following steps:

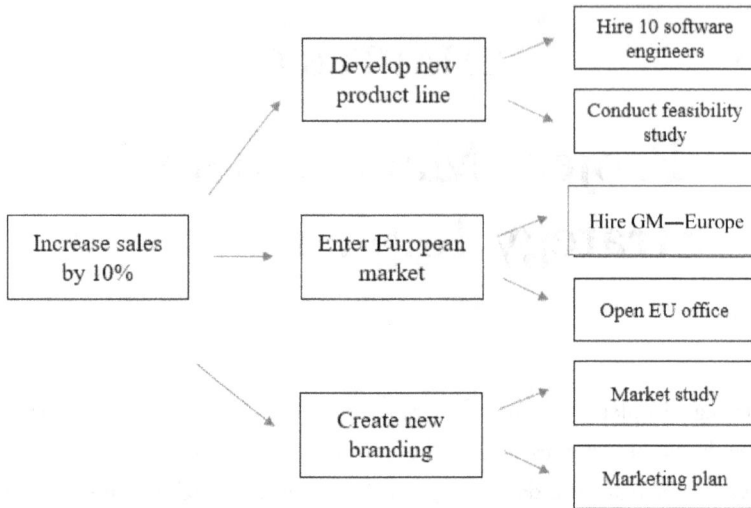

Figure 22 Cascading strategy implementation projects

1. Strategic statement of work (SSOW)

   The SSOW benefits from the use of SMART goals to identify tangible deliverables of strategic initiatives. Such goals are specific, measurable, attainable, relevant, and time bound. The term "relevant" in the case of the SSOW is in the sense that it may be traced back to the overriding strategy. The test of relevance assumes that a causal chain from strategy to initiative is understood. This relevance test is one that may only be carried out if the appropriate decision-making schemes such as systems thinking and root cause analysis have been conducted. When the reasoning associated with goal relevance is faulty, the strategic initiative will effectively solve the wrong problem. This in turn may lead to failure to implement the selected strategy or to cause the firm to veer off in an unintended strategic direction.

2. Strategic Initiative Charter

   The governing body of the firm responsible for the overall strategic planning effort issues the charter for each strategic initiative. The charter forms what some organizations refer to as "SITs" (Strategic Initiative [or Implementation] Teams), "PIPs" (Process Improvement [or Implementation] Projects), or other internal nomenclature. The purpose of the charter is the same as for charters developed for other projects within the firm. It identifies team members and includes a simple scope statement, high-level budget, and key milestones. The charter is important as it sends the message to the organization that the strategy of the company is being carried out in a formal manner. Therefore, with the charter assigned, the team has the authority to acquire resources, spend funding, and conduct the work of producing implementation-related deliverables. Finally, the act of officially chartering a strategic implementation team provides strong evidence that the firm is taking action to follow through on carrying out the selected strategy. This is important to gain buy-in and support from the stakeholders of the organization.

3. Strategic Initiative Risk Register

It is often said that companies do not fail because of the lack of good ideas fueling strategies, but rather, a failure to follow through and implement strategy. Many events can occur that derail strategy and strategic implementation. Such possible events are risks, and the risks that stand in the way of success must be identified and assessed so that the work of the strategic implementation team is not thrown off course. It is for this reason that the strategic implementation team identifies, assesses, and ranks the risks that are barriers to success to producing the chartered deliverables. The ranked risks are listed in the Strategic Initiative Risk Register and monitored and updated throughout the project. The impact of such risks is not only to the project itself, but to the success potential associated with carrying out the overall strategy (Figure 23).

While risk management is the explicit focus of the SIRR, it could be said additionally the Project-Led Strategic Management is a form of risk management. In the PLSM, each step is carefully identified, assessed for strengths and weaknesses, ranked in priority, and implemented. These steps correspond not only with the planning process but are also classic steps in the risk management process. The key for strategic risk management is to think through and closely manage plans for the development and implementation of strategy. Without such focus and attention to detail, the likelihood of drifting off

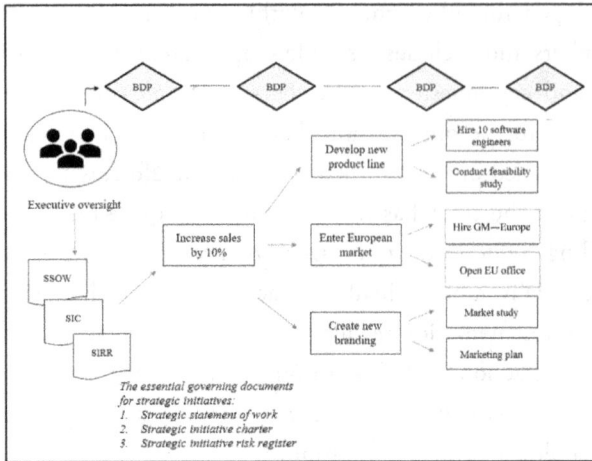

Figure 23 Oversight of cascading strategy projects

course increases. The factors that lead to drift are risks, and careful planning and aggressive management increase the chances of addressing those factors before they get in the way of goal achievement and the attaining of competitive advantage. At its core, PLSM is not only strategic management, but it is risk management.

4. Strategic Initiative Key Performance Indicators

How does the governing body of the organization determine the overall progress of strategic implementation and its associated strategic initiatives? This is done through the use of Key Performance Indicators. The Key Performance Indicators, or KPIs, represent the "M" or "Measurables" in the SMART goals emerging from the strategic implementation plan. While KPIs provide a high-level dashboard view of overall strategic progress, it is good practice to assign a KPI or an element of a KPI to each strategic implementation team. When this is done, as each project team tracks progress to plan, the data is fed to the overall strategic progress dashboard. This allows for tracking attainment of strategic waypoints at the executive level.

Project management practice also supports the measurement of ongoing progress of project deliverables so that the KPIs are informed by lower-level metrics. The primary metrics involve:

a. The budget for specific deliverables identified in work packages (also known as PV or Planned Value)

    b. The actual spending for specific deliverables identified in work packages (also known as AC or Actual Cost)

    c. The monetary value of work completed (also known as EV or Earned Value)

The three metrics associated with EVM or Earned Value Management provide an ideal means for ensuring that the bundle of activities identified in work packages and associated with strategic initiatives is closely tracked and managed. For example, each work package may be tracked using Earned Value Index. These include the SPI or Schedule Performance Index and the CPI or Cost Performance Index. The SPI tracks scheduled performance using the formula EV/PV. This formula informs schedule status by answering the question, "Is the monetary value of work that has been completed greater than, less than, or equal to that which was planned?" If EV is greater than PV, then more work was completed than planned and the SPI will be greater than 1. If EV is equal to PV, then the work is being completed as planned. If, however, PV is greater than EV, then work progress has fallen behind and the SPI will be less than 1.

    The Cost Performance Index works the same way but instead informs budget status by answering the question, "Is the monetary value of work that has been completed greater than, less than, or equal to the money actually spent?" If EV is greater than AC, then more work was completed than reflected in the money spent and the CPI will be greater than 1. If EV is equal to PV, then the work is being completed in line with spending. If, however, AC is greater than EV, then the project has spent more than the value of the work and the CPI will be less than 1.

EVM and KPIs?

How exactly do earned value metrics align with KPIs? Typically, a KPI will be linked to many underlying work packages. Therefore, each KPI will be flagged as "Red-Yellow-Green" accordingly, depending upon the collective EV metrics of the underlying work packages (Figure 24).

*Project and subproject
EV metrics cascade to
   KPI dashboard*

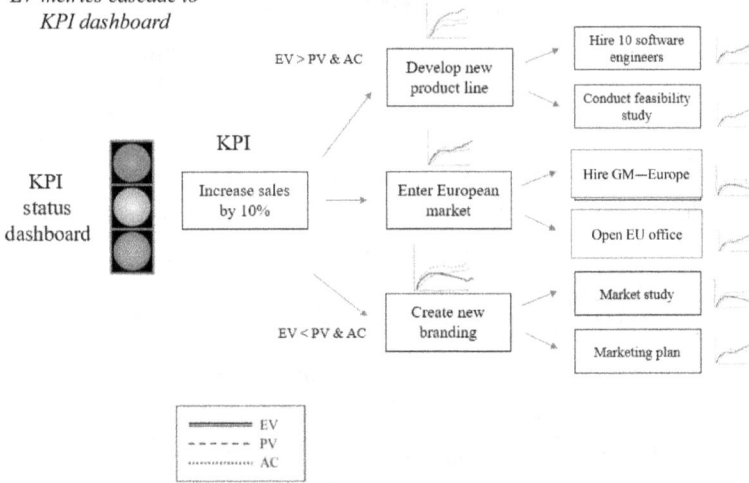

Figure 24 Earned value and KPIs

5. Strategic Initiative Governance Milestones

   Like other projects, strategic initiatives are managed in phases according to business decision points. The purpose of business decision points in project implementation is not only to gauge progress but to periodically reconfirm assumptions and validity of the initiative. For example, once a strategic initiative is chartered, its next step is to create a project plan. The plan requires resources, but not nearly as many resources as the plan implementation. It is the implementation of the plan that requires significant commitment of resources and budget. It is for this reason that a typical initial governance milestone occurs upon completion of the project plan. The plan is reviewed by the governing body so as to thoroughly vet the plan, its underlying assumptions, and its continued link to the overall strategy of the company. A successful business decision point leads to approval for the project to proceed to execution of the plan. Should questions arise regarding the plan that requires additional work, the strategic implementation team is redirected to carry out the additional analysis and return for an additional business decision point to confirm and approve the revised plan. It is possible that the charter of the team is no longer valid given the macroenvironment and the internal situation of the firm. In such a case, the project is terminated.

Governance milestones may also be called for an on ad hoc basis in the event that the project team encounters one or more possible situations:

a. The team requires major changes to previously agreed upon scope, schedule, and/or budget.

b. The team or governing body of the firm recognizes that the project as originally conceived is no longer feasible.

c. Obvious significant shifts in the internal and external macroenvironment have occurred.

d. Significant change requests have been put forward by stakeholders.

e. If none of the above conditions apply, the team continues to carry out the chartered project work until the previously agreed upon budget, scope, and schedule milestones have been reached.

6. Strategic Initiative Closure

The project closure process as outlined in the PMBOK applies to strategic initiative projects in the same way that it applies to any other project. Project closure is all about good housekeeping in that resources employed by the project are returned, contracts are terminated, and lessons learned are captured. There are no "loose ends" left hanging once the project ends when project closure is performed correctly. There are some key differences, however. The deliverables of a strategic initiative or implementation project contribute something lasting to the strategic profile of the company. This may involve new processes and procedures, the creation of plans, the implementation of a new organization structure, or some other tangible artifact to be included in the ongoing operation. This puts a stronger emphasis on the handover of the deliverables to the ongoing operation. This may involve significant training and perhaps a pilot run of the deliverables. In some cases, a separate project may be chartered to lead the transfer of deliverables and piloting of their usage in the organization. If this strategy is implemented, the existing project is closed, the new project is chartered, and the new project closes once the ongoing operation has fully incorporated the deliverables. The chartering of the separate handover project makes sense if the scale of the handover and incorporation of the processes warrant the additional focus and support (Figure 25).

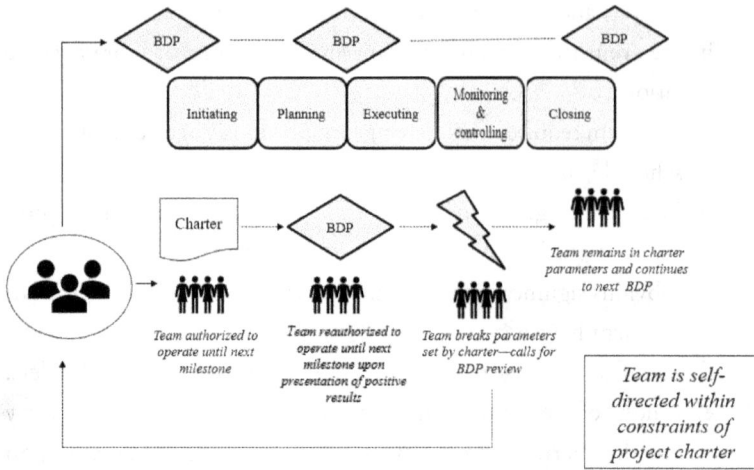

Figure 25 Governance milestone management

Portfolio, Program, and Project

It is not uncommon for firms to have many strategic implementation projects chartered and in various stages of execution at the same. This is in addition to the many projects associated with product development efforts. It could be said that much of the work of the firm gets done by projects and very little is accomplished through ongoing operations. One example of this is the tendency for most firms today to focus on the development of products and services while outsourcing operational components such as manufacturing, some internal services such as recruiting and payroll, and, finally, elements of the supply chain. The increasing focus on projects to manage work, including the development and implementation of strategy, has led to the understanding of the firm through the lens of projects, programs, and portfolios (PPP). Any work—be it strategic or operational in nature—that is temporary, unique, complex, and employs resources is defined as a project. Very large projects or a group of related projects is often referred to as a program. For example, in strategic management, the firm may charter a project to design a new logo, a project to craft a new marketing communications plan, and, finally, a project to implement a new customer relationship management (CRM) application. Together these projects could form the Marketing Revitalization *Program.* Finally, the total of all projects and programs for which the company invests is referred to as the company *Portfolio* of project and program investments. Because projects, programs, and the portfolio form the bulk of what the modern firm does, the study of firms using this lens is referred to as PPP.

PPP as Tiered Management

The alignment of project management with strategic management has been recognized by practitioners who envision an ongoing enterprise managed in tiers using project management practices. At the highest tier of management lies the company portfolio consisting of the total spending on project investments. Programs exist at the second management tier and are defined as collections of related projects or initiatives. Projects are temporary endeavors that produce deliverables, including products and services, for external offerings as well as internal strategic initiatives. The thinking behind the "PPP" or "Portfolio, Program, and Project" model is that the top-level strategy of the company cascades from strategic portfolio decisions to the management of collections of projects related to specific areas of strategic focus within the firm, to tangible efforts to produce specific deliverables at the project level (Figure 26).

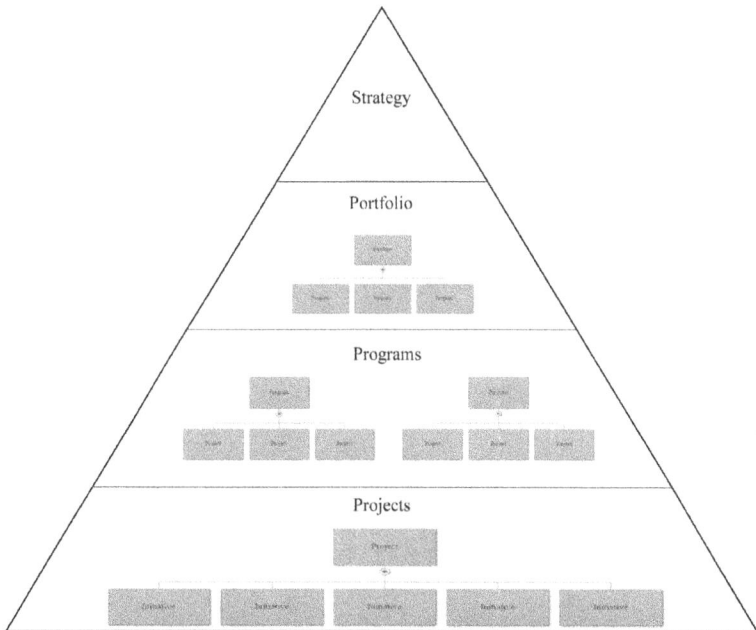

Figure 26 Strategy, portfolio, program, and projects

Although this operational concept has gained in popularity, it has as its primary focus the set of activities within the firm that are managed as projects. For example, the PPP model is usually focused on deliverables to stakeholders outside of the company and the associated management of complexity that comes with it. The model does not necessarily apply project management practice to the analysis, formula, choice, and implementation framework employed within strategic management. However, there is a natural fit. The strategic planning process in the case of a PPP managed organization becomes linked with project management in the overall governance of the firm. The company charters projects to evaluate the current portfolio of programs and projects to assess the degree that they are fulfilling strategic goals and positioning the firm for competitiveness. Monitoring and control tools adopted from project management practice are used to assess the status of programs and projects in process. Further, given the principle of "sunk costs," an effective governance system uses project selection tools periodically to "reselect" ongoing projects as necessary to ensure that they remain in alignment with the mission of the company. The project management mindset is therefore ideal for bringing process focus to an important responsibility of senior managers that may otherwise be managed in an unsystematic manner. Finally, the highest tier of PPP involves the governance committee or board that charters all projects, tracks resources assigned and available to be assigned throughout all projects and programs, and, finally, oversees the business decision points within the phases of project and program management.

Strategic Implementation Example

Consider the strategic initiative to increase sales by 10 percent. Further, assume that this initiative is one of many associated with a high-level strategy. Project management practice indicates that a project begins with a charter and with the identification of stakeholders.

Strategic Initiative Charter

Stakeholders for the initiative include an array of internal and external interested parties. To name but a few:

1. *Employees*: Employees could be considered a single stakeholder category, yet some employees will have stronger interests than others. For example, increasing sales will naturally require additional salespeople. Some employees may have interest in such jobs, while some existing salespeople may express concern. As an example, what happens to existing sales territories and quotas when additional sales personnel are added? Also, employees within functional groups that support sales such as manufacturing, material control, and supply chain management will have concerns. Additional ramp-up of sales will require a response in terms of supply. This may in turn require additional supporting employees or perhaps longer hours. Employees therefore are a stakeholder category that will benefit from scrutiny.

2. *Customers*: Customers are another example of a large stakeholder group with varied interests. Current customers may expect that the company seeking an increase in sales will press customers for additional volume. Often customers do not wish to "put all eggs in one basket" and will be reluctant to increase the share of total purchase volume to any given supplier. A proposal from a supplier to do so will likely lead to the extraction of additional benefits such as pricing or improved terms. Customers who see the attempt to increase sales by acquiring other customers or new markets may have concerns about the possibility of defocus within a key supplier. This could lead to some major customers "pulling away" and reducing the existing business volume in light of such concerns. The initiative to increase sales must be careful not to trigger a situation where unintended consequences occur.

3. *Competitors*: Competitors play within the same market, so they are impacted by the strategic moves of competition. Will the move for one company to increase sales impinge upon the market share currently enjoyed by the competition? While this may or may not occur, the important issue is that competitors may believe that this is likely to occur and begin immediate competitive countermeasures. Competitors are therefore a stakeholder group with significant power to derail a proposed strategic initiative. It is recommended that they be given a high priority in stakeholder analysis and treated with caution.

4. *Shareholders*: The interest of shareholders in the outcome of the project is magnified by virtue of their ownership stake in the company. Increased sales is naturally desirable. However, the question arises, "To what degree does the increase in sales translate to increased profitability?" There is wisdom in this question. Company shareholders understand that increased sales will likely involve increased risk to one degree or another. For example, additional sales require new investments in employees and infrastructure that lead to additional fixed cost. Additional sales could also require investment in the development of new products that is likely to be significant. Finally, additional sales could require that the firm pursue new markets and will likely inspire countermeasures from competitors. An in-depth stakeholder analysis therefore will benefit from assessing the thinking of shareholders and determine which of these require the most steering toward buy-in of the strategic initiative (Figure 27).

Once the stakeholder analysis has been conducted and the charter created and authorized, the next step is to develop the scope of the strategic initiative. The scope outlines in detail exactly what it is that the chartered initiative will deliver. This is an important focus for strategic management.

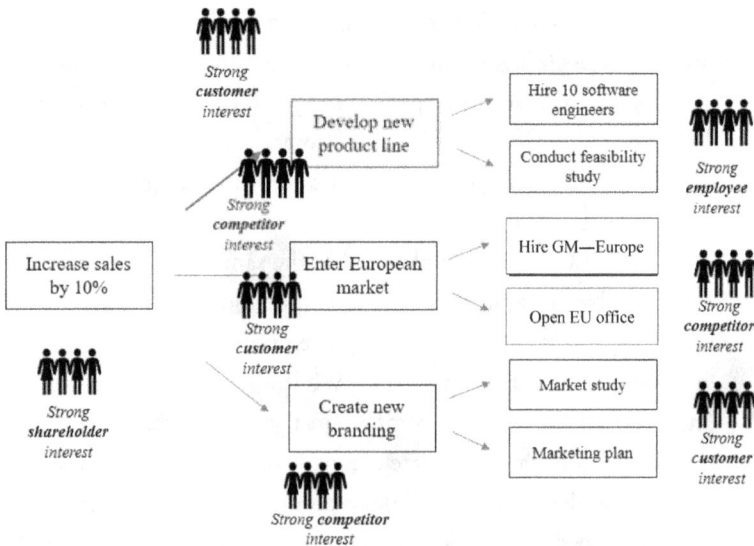

Figure 27 Strategy implementation stakeholders

It is not enough to develop strategic ideas, but rather, the delivery of tangible results—with the ultimate goal in mind of achieving a sustained competitive advantage. The clear definition of scope therefore focuses the team carrying out the initiative on specific outcomes (Figure 28).

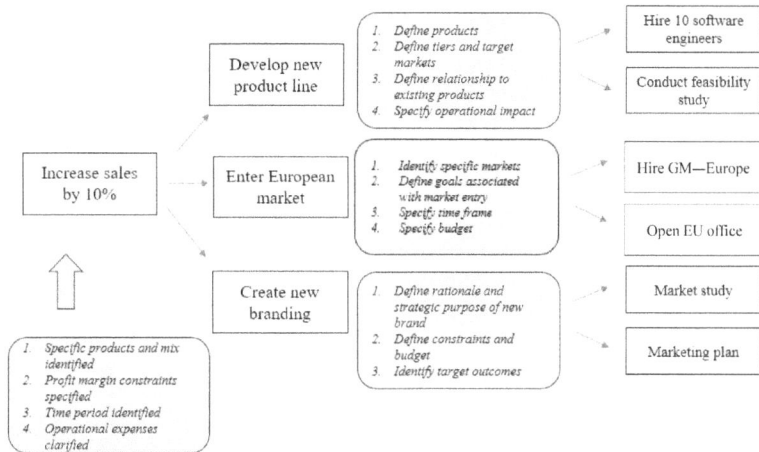

Figure 28 Scope detailed in strategic implementation

Beyond Scope and Charter

The scope answers the question, "What?"—specifically—"What will we deliver?" Once it is clear what the strategic initiative will deliver and who the players are within and outside the organization, the next step in the strategic initiative is to answer questions such as:

"When will this initiative be complete?"

"How much will this cost?"

"Who can we assign to the initiative?"

"What level of performance will be required?" (or, "How high will the quality level need to be?")

"What progress and status information will need to be communicated to stakeholders?"

"What barriers to success can we anticipate?"

"What outside assistance will be needed to carry out this initiative?", and, finally,

"What internal or external partners might we need to collaborate with?"

Experienced project managers will immediately recognize that the answers to these questions are provided by the project subplans that are outlined by the 10 knowledge areas within the Project Management Body of Knowledge framework. By inspection, every aspect of the strategic initiative is guided by detailed plans so that the close management associated with focused execution is assured (Figure 29).

Subplan	Questions answered by each subplan
Integration	How will we tie together all elements of the project plan?
Scope	What exactly will we deliver?
Time	When will we deliver it?
Cost	How much will it cost?
Quality	What performance level of deliverables is expected?
Human resources	Who will do the work?
Comms.	How will information and progress be reported?
Risk	What difficulties do we anticipate?
Procure	What elements of strategic deliverables will be outsourced?
Stakeholder	Who are the players in the overall project community?

Figure 29 Questions answered by subplans

Executing strategic initiative in this manner provides for additional focus on the mechanics of carrying out the activity. The project management process framework provides senior management increased visibility into the efforts to create a comprehensive plan, apply resources, budget, and monitor and control the plan. It can be concluded that managing strategic initiatives as projects improves the chances of success and leaves little to chance.

Control within Strategy Implementation

It has been said that firms do not fail because of a lack of ideas, rather they fail because they fail to implement those ideas. It is therefore one thing to develop a strategic initiative, but quite another to ensure its success. The strategic management process does not offer a tangible methodology for continually checking the progress of strategic initiatives and then acting to ensure that they remain on track. The Monitoring and Controlling process group within the PMBOK, however, does provide a methodology for evaluating the progress of a project or initiative, comparing the progress to plan, and then taking specific actions to adjust the plan to recover. Strategic initiatives may at times lose focus and begin to move in directions not initially intended. Also, some strategic initiatives tend to begin strong and then "fizzle." What strategic initiatives may be missing are the underlying elements for executing and controlling projects that are employed in good project management practice. For example, a strategic initiative managed as a project is managed with a complete plan that includes a scope, schedule, and budget baseline. The baseline represents a fixed commitment for what the initiative will deliver, when it will deliver it, and how much it will cost. The leader of the strategic management tracks the progress of each initiative, compares it to the baseline, and then acts to bring the project back into compliance.

The baseline provides another important function beyond monitoring and control. The baseline works to ensure that the project avoids the temptation to drift into areas not originally included in the project charter. This additional control function is the change control process. Once the baseline of the project/initiative is set, any changes to the baseline require the submission and evaluation of a change request (Figure 30).

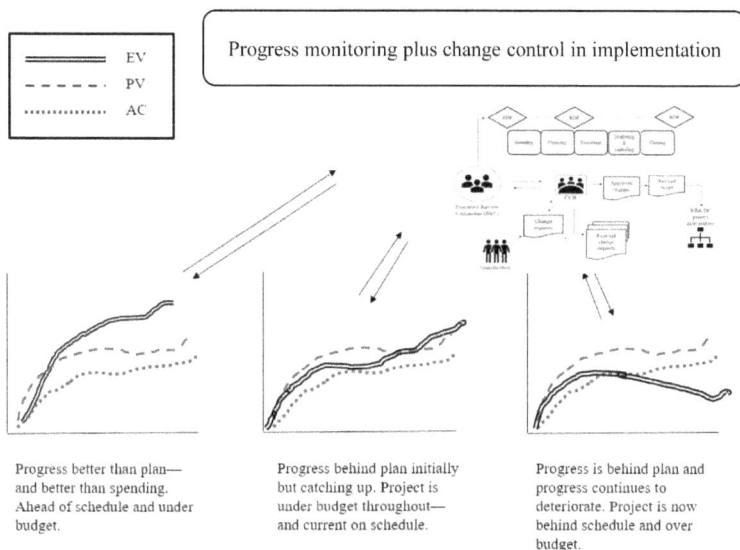

Figure 30 Progress monitoring and change control

In the context of implementing strategy using strategic initiatives, changes to the scope, schedule, or budget of the initiative are presented to senior management for evaluation. Using this method borrowed from project management practice, strategic initiatives are closely managed and controlled at the highest levels of the company.

Summary of Observations

Strategic management and project management are characterized by a sequence of steps. Project management, like strategic management, seeks to link action to strategic focus. It is also observed that strategic initiatives are projects as they fit the definition of what constitutes a project. However, although project management practice is tightly defined by standards and supporting certification, approaches to strategic management is observed to vary between firms. While the need for tangible goals, defined practices, and standard decision-making techniques is recognized as being important to strategic management, business practice in these areas is observed to be applied inconsistently (Table 2).

Table 2 Project management and strategic management

Project Management	Strategic Management
Process steps: Initiating, planning, executing, monitoring and controlling, closing	Process steps: Analysis, formulation, choice, implementation
Formal authorization (charter)	Observed to be inconsistent in application across firms
Tangible deliverables and outcomes	Often lacking and cited as cause of strategic management problems
Defined management practices	Lack of universally defined management practices in strategic management process
Decision-making tools	Inconsistent application of decision-making methods
Projects	Initiatives
Links actions to strategy	Links actions to strategy

The gap between the unfulfilled requirements of strategic management and the capabilities of project management practices suggests that companies could benefit from using project management to fill gaps in current strategy development and implementation. It is envisioned that the coupling between project management and strategic management becomes seamless. Project management simply becomes the "set of business processes for getting work done." Perhaps this definition does not include all work carried out by the organization—but it fits most cases from product development to system development and implementation to marketing campaigns. It is also observed to be a strong fit in the domain of strategic planning and implementation. For this reason, the complete system could be envisioned as PLSM—or "Project-Led Strategic Management."

PART 2

Implementing a Project-Led Strategic Management System

While the management of strategy employing the mechanism of project management as well as the PPP-tiered approach to manage is observed to offer benefits, not all companies have implemented this approach. Firms that do not currently employ such an approach to its management may well wonder how and where to begin on the journey to a project management–led strategic development and implementation framework. A move to this type of organization is in itself a strategic planning management project characterized by the following steps:

1. Assessment of the current state
2. Identification of future desired state
3. Identification of gaps: current versus future
4. Phases of implementation of the future state
5. Creation of Phase 0 infrastructure
6. Pilot run of Phase 0
7. Lessons learned and preparation of following phase
8. Implementation of continuous improvement mechanisms

CHAPTER 7

The Current and Future State

Strategy is aspirational in nature. It outlines where the company seeks to go as well as what position it seeks to occupy in the market. Successfully arriving at the strategic destination requires a sound understanding of the current position of the company as well as the distance to be travelled to reach the desired position. This is accomplished by determining the current state, the desired future state, and, finally, the gaps that separate. Chapter 7 introduces this method for understanding how to reach the desired strategic destination.

A firm that does not currently employ project management for the development and implementation of strategy may not yet have established a structured approach to strategy development. Management of the strategic waypoints using project management is not possible if the underlying structure is not yet in place. Determining the current position of the company will therefore require some initial investigation. The change management literature offers guidance on where to begin using techniques for the diagnosis of the initial state. This is carried out by various means of data collection, including the following:

A) Collection and analysis of archival records: Historical data of financial, operational, and strategic trends, and also timelines of key strategic initiatives, successes, and serious challenges.
B) Collection and review of any existing company documentation of processes, procedure, and organizational structure.
C) Interviewing key stakeholders within the organization: Key contributors drawn from all levels of the organization and interviewed using a standard set of questions vetted by the executive governance committee. Each interview is recorded.

D) Documenting the outcome of stakeholder interviews: Recorded interviews are transcribed for analysis by using either software or specialist assigned to the tasks.

E) Analysis of collected data: Themes are extracted from interview transcripts using techniques such as qualitative data analysis (QDA), algorithmic text mining, or a combination of both.

F) Validation of analysis using focus groups, survey instruments, or a combination of the above. Validation is important for the purpose of comparing and contrasting findings derived from any single data source. Validation involves triangulation of multiple sources to arrive at a holistic understanding of the situation.

The result of the assessment of the current state therefore provides an understanding of the organizational baseline. The results are communicated to all employees to maximize stakeholder understanding of the current situation with the goal in mind of securing buy-in from the population of employees. The analysis will also lay the groundwork for the demonstration of the need for a new system.

Identification of Future Desired State

The vision of a future of a company that organizes its strategic planning around a structured methodology and incorporating project management practices is likely to be overwhelming. Recall that at this stage, the important outcome is to clearly identify what would need to be in place if the company were going to operate a project management–led strategic planning process. The components that must exist to operate such an organization and process would include:

1. *Governance Body*: This is the committee of executives that charter projects, assign project managers, and rule on governance milestone evaluations.

2. *Project Manager*: The implementation of a project-led strategic planning organization is in itself a project. While the components required to run projects may not likely exist, the project manager in the early stage of implementation could identify missing pieces and propose them as subprojects to the governance body for approval.

3. *Policy Framework*: A traditional functional organization complemented by an ad hoc strategic planning system may require few policies, procedures,

and guidelines. The chain of command is clear, and subordinates report and take direction from the next level of management. A project, program, and portfolio organization has the potential to be more effective, but implementing it does require additional supporting guidelines.

The three components associated with the desired future state appear straightforward and common to most organizations. However, each could be thought of as a collection of subprojects—each of which could be broken down into further detail. For example, the governance body is more than a collection of executives. Executives who play a role in the governance of projects must understand what their respective roles are. Grouping together executives in a decision-making team does not ensure that they understand what decisions need to be made, when, and how the team interacts with chartered project teams. Further, the ability to make decisions at the executive level assumes that the right data exists to support such decision-making activity. Financial- and corporate-level strategy may be relatively clear, and operational data on the performance of the company will likely be available to the team. However, other key inputs to decision making such as a resource histogram may be missing. These issues illustrate that the identification of the need for a governance body in the future state of the company does not stop at the creation of the body itself, but also includes components such as:

A) Training
B) Policies and procedures
C) Information system updates
D) Political and cultural changes

Identification of Gaps

Where is the right place to start when the new organization requires policies, procedures, guidelines—all with an accompanying new structure? The first small step may involve not WHAT but WHO. This is because the knowledge required to identify gaps between the existing and future state of the firm will require deep knowledge on how a project management–led strategic management organization operates. This knowledge either may not exist in the current organization or it exists only in embryonic form. While internal individuals may exist who are strong at leading process improvement initiatives, an outside consultant with appropriate know-how is usually required to fill in knowledge gaps, introduce the new concepts to the organization, and steer the project so that it is focused on the right goals. Outside expertise may aid in identifying gaps. This is why it is important to consider WHO will provide leadership and guidance for the effort from either inside or outside of the organization. This begins with the definition of a "Gap." The simplest definition of a gap is that it is a missing piece that, if filled, would result in at least one element of the desired future state. The gap analysis therefore is the identification of the scope of the process improvement project. Each gap is a deliverable that may also include many subdeliverables. The project manager then proceeds to identify gap deliverables and subdeliverables one by one in a way that leads ultimately to a process improvement work breakdown structure (WBS) that defines the scope to be delivered in the project to implement a project-led strategic management organization.

Phased Implementation

What then unfolds after the gap analysis? In short, what happens next is the same series of steps that occur within any project. The project manager, outside consultant, and any assigned project team members identify the activities required to produce the deliverables collected in the project WBS (Figure 31).

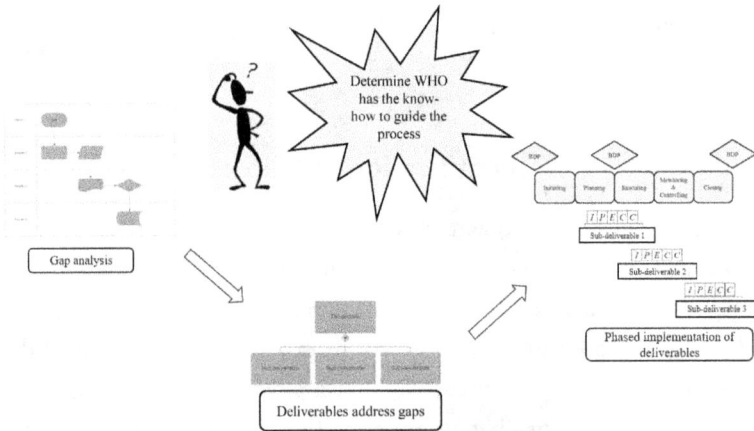

Figure 31 Implementation from gaps to deliverables

Incorporating the New System

Instilling a new way of doing things into a company is a long-term endeavor that involves a change in culture, the incorporation of knowledge management, and, finally, exercising and improving systems over time so that it becomes "second nature." This is what is referred to as maturity.

CHAPTER 8

Changing the Culture

While companies aspire to bigger and better things in the pursuit of a competitive advantage, at the same time, stability is desirable for ongoing operational efficiency. The culture of the company is an important stabilizing factor as it reinforces the identity of the company as well as its way of doing things. A strong culture, however, may become a challenge when it becomes clear that the strategy and direction of the company needs to change. Chapter 8 introduces ideas for how to shift the culture so that it becomes a better fit for the new strategy.

Implementing project-led strategic management requires a new way of doing things as well as a new way of thinking. Instead of taking action in an ad hoc fashion, the employees of the firm now must stop and think prior to "doing" and engage with the newly established process. It takes time, however, to implement a new system as it involves many intangible factors involving people, communication, processes, tools, as well as the interaction between levels and groups within the organization. Also, it is common for many companies to look back on the founders of the company as well as key employees who went "above and beyond" to take actions that saved the company. These could range from desperate overnight work on a product deliverable essential for the sustained operation of the company or solving a critical problem just in time to prevent the company from failing. While "hero" stories are positive and provide examples for employees to rally around, they are symptomatic of the use of ad hoc methods within the company. Ad hoc methods, or "doing what apparently needs to be done as a reaction to internal or external triggers," are the antithesis of a process-led organization. Process-focused firms employ a systematic approach. They "plan first, then do." They seek to produce repeatable and reliable results. Repeatable and reliable results cannot be guaranteed by ad hoc methods, nor can the development of strategy followed by a robust strategic implementation. These are a function of a process-focused organization that employs a systematic approach to competitive advantage, the achievement of strategic milestones, customer satisfaction, and return on investment (ROI).

Many models exist for managing and implementing change. Such models could be employed in the endeavor to shift the company in the direction of a new process-focused culture. Regardless of the model selected to foster change, most have elements that are universally observed in managing change. These elements are described as follows:

1. Breaking with the status quo

   The universal first step in managing change toward a new culture is the recognition that a change is needed. In many cases, business results and major shifts in the macroenvironment inform the company that the current approach to doing business is simply not sufficient for long-term success. In other cases, there may not be an obvious need to change. When this is the case, the "if it ain't broke, don't fix it" attitude is likely to be present. It takes strong leadership and effective communication to break through and achieve an understanding that a change in culture is needed, and the time to change is "now."

2. Rallying around the mission

   Change is best carried out when the stakeholders of the organization are firmly behind the initiative and are willing to make sacrifices and offer unqualified support. Many approaches to fostering this mindset are cited in the literature. In practice, leaders of the culture change initiative involve stakeholders in crafting the new vision and developing the plan. Further, they are quick to communicate the essence of "what's in it for me?" at every opportunity when interacting with stakeholder groups. There is an old saying that "you can't push on a string." With this in mind, stakeholders are drawn in by making the vision of the new culture highly attractive.

3. Taking action

   Change is implemented by chartering projects that implement the components seen to support and evolve the new culture. While the emphasis in culture change initiatives often focuses on the preparation and lead-in to action, eventually the gears of change need to mesh and produce tangible results from strategic initiative projects.

4. Permanent adoption

Will the culture change initiatives produce lasting change? Or, will the new culture regress and revert back to what existed previously? Organizations are observed to have "organizational inertia" and either resist change or revert back to a more familiar, comfortable state. This is known to occur when business and Enterprise Resource Planning systems are implemented in firms. Some firms seek to implement and permanently adopt change by implementing new advanced systems that incorporate best practices that have evolved industrywide over the years. Unfortunately, many firms are not able to resist modifying new systems so that the systems emulate existing internal processes rather than new practices. When this happens, it is all too easy to regress back to "square one" after spending significant time and money. Regression is to be avoided, and the new culture is one that will remain in place even as management and employees change. Incorporating a new system while employees come and go over time requires intensive focus on the part of management. The challenge is also one of knowledge management (Figure 32).

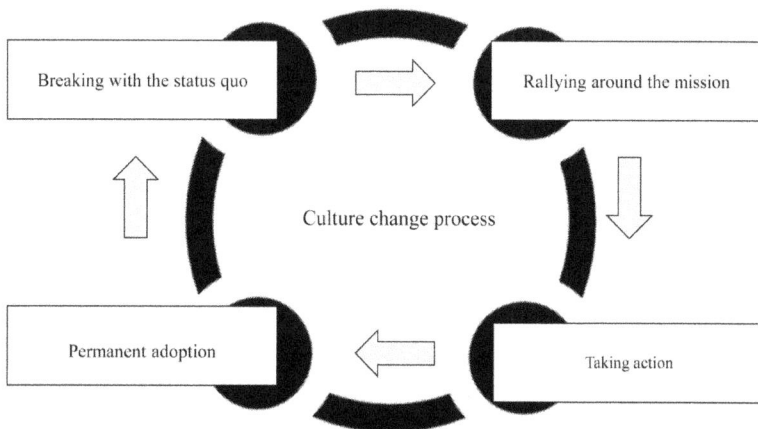

Figure 32 The culture change process

Finally, it could be argued that project-led strategic management inherently draws stakeholders into the strategic management process. When each element of the strategic management process is broken down into manageable pieces and chartered as projects, resources are drawn from the functional groups of the company and duly assigned. Multiple projects require significant resources to work on strategic initiatives. This is a means for developing increased involvement among the stakeholder population as well as driving communication and discussion of strategic activities throughout the company.

CHAPTER 9

Knowledge Management: What Is It?

Knowledge resides within the minds of employees. However, employees come and go throughout the life of the company. It is desirable that knowledge resides within the company in a manner that does not necessarily depend upon the know-how of specific individuals. This is especially important in the case of a process-focused organization and is a must in the case of project-led strategic management implementation. Chapter 9 describes the process of acquiring, recording, retaining, and incorporating knowledge through the knowledge management process.

"Knowledge management" is a widely used, but often misunderstood, word. One of the reasons for this is that it is a term that refers to a broad spectrum of activities within the organization. It does not refer to one thing, but many things. To illustrate this, consider the example of a manager directing an employee to implement knowledge management within the organization. How would this be done? Where would an employee begin to start "doing knowledge management"?

Understanding the construct of knowledge management requires first understanding what is meant by the term "knowledge." One way to approach this is by the use of the DIKW or "Data, Information, Knowledge, Wisdom" framework drawn from information technology practice and introduced as part of the theoretical underpinnings of the data collection and reporting model of the PMBOK beginning with version 5. It is important to notice that knowledge is something that emerges over time beginning with the acquisition of data. **Data** is raw and unrefined samples of the macroenvironment. For example, data collected from grocery store cash registers provides a mass of collected transactions. However, the data itself is not necessarily meaningful nor relevant. It takes the application of work in the form of performing analysis to extra meaning and relevant **information**. Data is therefore acquired, and information is that relevant detail extracted from the irrelevant "noise" so that managers may be informed so that action may be taken. **Knowledge** emerges from the application and use of the information extracted from data. Finally, **wisdom** is that which emerges from internalized institutional application of knowledge over time.

The DIKW model illustrates how knowledge is developed within an organization and is characterized by the following steps:

1. Data is acquired
2. Data is analyzed
3. Information is extracted from data
4. Information is applied
5. Knowledge emerges

This five-step sequence could be characterized as:

Acquisition, Analysis, Extraction, Application, Emergence (AAEAE Process)

When organizations seek to manage knowledge, they seek to develop knowledge within the firm and retain it. When the term "knowledge management" is used in the organization, it primarily refers to the retention of knowledge. Since knowledge emerges from the action taken by employees to act upon information, knowledge frequently resides in the brains of employees. Such knowledge is referred to as **tacit knowledge**. The goal of knowledge management is to extract knowledge from employees into a form that remains with the organization even after the employee with the knowledge leaves the company. This requires that knowledge be documented in some way. Knowledge that is documented is known as **explicit knowledge**. What managers really mean when they use the term "knowledge management" is "to actively convert tacit knowledge to explicit knowledge so that the organization retains knowledge formerly held only by the employee."

How then is knowledge management implemented? It is often done in stages as knowledge management practice within the organization matures. Here is one example of steps to consider when implementing such a process for use in a project-led strategic management system. (Note: This process assumes that knowledge has already emerged from the acquisition of data and extraction of information such that the employees involved have the knowledge under consideration.) Also, each step includes the relevant questions that the action taken will answer.

Phase 1: Documentation of Processes

Process flows:

- What triggers the formation of a strategic project team?
- What steps are taken (and by whom) for forming a project team?
- How are proposals created and delivered to the executive decision-making committee?
- How is a project team chartered? Who issues the charter?
- How are project charters communicated?
- How are resources acquired for each project?
- How are project funds allocated?
- What is the process for accounting for the cost of resources?

Formulas:

- How are estimates developed?
- How are resource costs calculated?
- How is project progress measured?
- How is progress toward strategic waypoints measured?
- How are KPIs measured and reported?

Work instructions:

- What steps are required for entering and exiting each project phase?
- What specific internal data sources are used for data collection purposes?
- What tools are used for analyzing and reporting on collected data?

Rules of thumb:

- What known undocumented approaches to carrying out work or solving problems exist in the organization?

Practices:

- What norms exist within each functional group that are applied in the course of doing work within a discipline?
- What tacit practices must be captured and documented?

Technical procedures:

- What steps are undertaken when performing technical operations?
- What tacit processes exist that are best understood by only a few key people?

Phase 2: Formalizing Documented Process

Templates:

- What existing reports, requests, or procedures would benefit with the use of a standard template?
- What categories of templates are needed to support the new processes associated with project-led strategic management?

Checklists:

- What processes, practices, or deliverables would benefit from systematic confirmation?
- Who has the know-how that would provide the content associated with checklists?

Embedded workflows:

- What internal processes are known to be error prone and would benefit from establishing an embedded workflow?

- What new processes are needed that should be adapted into embedded workflows?

Processes coded into business systems:

- Do current business systems support the new proposed processes?
- What additional systems, new systems, or modifications to existing systems are required to support new processes?

White papers:

- What internal trade secrets and proprietary methods currently exist that lack formal documentation?
- What formal documents currently exist that synthesize research results and internal know-how?

Instruction manuals:

- What current instruction manuals exist to support work processes?
- What instruction manuals are in need of development to support new processes?

Phase 3: Storage of Documented Knowledge

Intranet:

- Where are work products from strategic projects stored?
- Who has access to artifacts such as strategic analysis, formulation, and recommendation reports?

Central server:

- What infrastructure is in place to support the data and application needs of the project team?
- What additions to the existing infrastructure will be required to support the new systems?

Cloud-based storage:
- Will the company use internal company-owned hardware or will cloud systems be employed for data storage, retrieval, and analysis?
- Which, if any, cloud system providers provide the required features and supporting architecture?

Library:
- How are documented resources and media categorized for ease of retrieval?
- What media will be used to document the array of artifacts associated with the knowledge base of the company?

File organization:
- What file and directory nomenclature is required to foster the maintenance of stored documentation in an orderly manner?

Phase 4: Retrieval of Documented Knowledge

Document retrieval system:
- How do employees find the information needed?
- What new retrieval processes and technology are required to support the growing volume of documentation and media?

Search engine:
- What search engine technology will be used for internal documentation and media search?
- What search engine technology is recommended for external documentation and media search?

Workstation templates:
- Do current employee PCs use standard desktop templates pointing to the Intranet front page?
- Is it foreseen that new processes require desktop standardization?

Dashboards:
- How will KPIs associated with the new processes be displayed?
- What data will dashboards contain?

Security:

- Who has access to documents and media stored in the knowledge management system?
- What clearance levels will be required to support the system?
- How will security be maintained when knowledge systems are accessed remotely?

It is observed that the implementation of knowledge management is a multilayered highly nuanced exercise. The questions posed in the implement steps represent initial suggestions. These initial questions are likely to lead to others, which is why the term "knowledge management" is in fact a complex construct rather than a simple action that is performed (Figure 33).

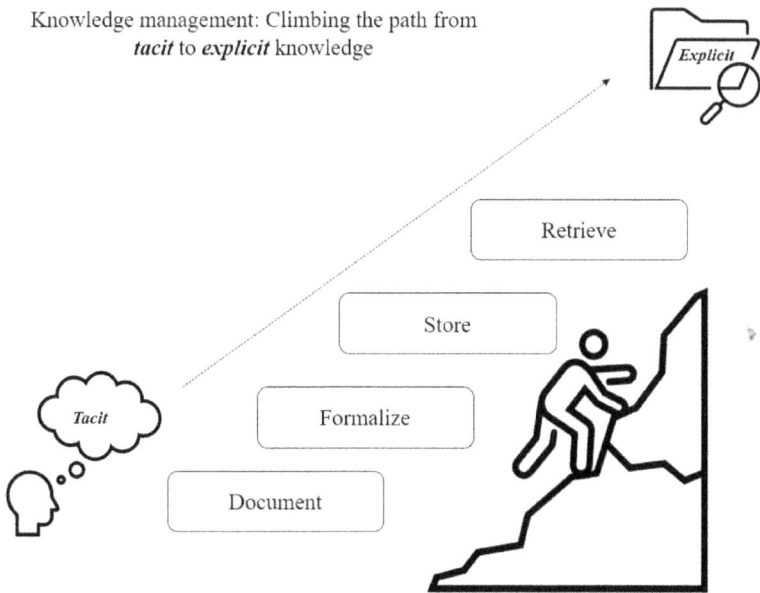

Knowledge management: Climbing the path from *tacit* to *explicit* knowledge

Explicit

Retrieve

Store

Tacit

Formalize

Document

Figure 33 From tacit to explicit knowledge

CHAPTER 10

Knowledge Management, Project Management, and Maturity

The concept of knowledge management is embedded within project management practice with the practice of collecting, reviewing, storing, and converting "lessons learned" in organizational process assets. Leadership employing project-led strategic management can freely draw upon project management to advance knowledge management. Further, the optimization of practices, as well as knowledge collection, results in the maturing of the organization from a process perspective. These ideas are introduced and explained in Chapter 10.

The guide to the project management body of knowledge has long included the capture of "lessons learned" throughout the project followed by a review of lessons learned at the end of the project along with documentation of lessons learned for future use. The "lessons learned" process could be viewed as a rudimentary form of knowledge management that is now further formalized in the sixth edition of the PMBOK. The processes associated with "Manage Project Knowledge" in the PMBOK are focused not only on lessons learned but also on the institutionalization of knowledge. Tacit knowledge that is transformed into explicit knowledge and becomes a way of life becomes in PMBOK terms "Organizational Process Assets." Further, the application of knowledge in project management could be viewed as what the PMBOK describes as **expert judgment**. Expert judgment is often applied by project managers when **making decisions**. Over time, the practice applying knowledge as expert judgment in decision making leads to better decision results, and those project managers who can do this provide us with examples of the emergence of **wisdom**. The goal for project management maturity in any given organization is to take what stakeholders think and do as well as the know-how they apply in their work and transform it over time into Organizational Process Assets. This process is one of continuous improvement and the development of maturity as an organization.

Maturing the System

It is observed that the attainment of knowledge and wisdom is a moving target. What constitutes knowledge today may in 20 or 30 years (or sooner!) become irrelevant. To continue to employ the best practices for project-led strategic management requires not only the focus on the activities carried out but rather the overall system of processes being employed. The ability to manage the complex systems involved and optimize them is not something that occurs overnight. Instead, it evolves slowly over the long term as processes are exercised and holes in execution. It involves people, processes, and infrastructure working seamlessly together. Using a comparison with human development, the process of managing processes, from KM to the complete support of project-led strategic management, could be thought of as the "Sit, Stand, Walk, Run" framework described next.

Table 3 Inputs, tools and techniques, outputs

Inputs	Tools and Techniques	Outputs

1. Project management plan
  • All components
2. Project documents
  • Lessons learned register
  • Program team assignments
  • Resource breakdown structure
  • Stakeholder register
3. Deliverables
4. Enterprise Environmental factors
5. Organizational process assets
	1. Expert judgment
	2. Knowledge management
	3. Information management
	4. Interpersonal and team skills
	  • Active listening
	  • Facilitation
	  • Leadership
	  • Networking
	  • Political awareness
		1. Lessons learned register
		2. Project management plan updates
		  • Any component
		3. Organizational process assets updates

Sit

Strategic planning and implementation occur but does so using ad hoc methods, or via "methods du jour" introduced at different levels of the organization. The planning and implementation process is not managed as a series of closely managed projects. Finally, strategic success evaluation methods, such as profitability or the attainment of competitive advantage, tend to be "hit or miss."

Stand

Project-led strategic management is introduced to the organization. The governance body is instituted, and the first pilot projects are chartered. The process "goes live" in a strategic planning cycle after the successful execution of the pilot run.

Walk

All employees are made aware of the project-led strategic management methodology. Employees and management exercise rudimentary processes for implementing the new system. The initial policies, procedures, and infrastructure are put in place to support the new system. The phased implementation of knowledge management for the purpose of developing and storing organizational process assets begins. Key Performance Indicators for the process are tracked for the purpose of progress measurement of strategic projects as well as for the purpose of evaluating the benefits of the process.

Run

The process is exercised for multiple cycles. Knowledge management and other supporting infrastructure are fully implemented. Data is collected from each cycle and analyzed for process disconnects as well as effectiveness. Strategic initiative projects are chartered to address observed flaws and limitations within the system. The project-led strategic management system and supporting infrastructure is observed to be optimized over time (Figure 34).

Ad hoc methods are employed.   Processes are defined.   Processes are implemented.   Processes are shared, communicated, and optimized.

Sit   Stand   Walk   Run

Figure 34 Maturing the system

PART 3

Observing the System at Work: A Case Study

One way to consider the merits of PLSM is to consider a case of a failed product development and launch that was a result of unclear strategy, weak implementation, and short-sighted follow through. It is no surprise that such an approach to the market and accompanying strategy would result in missing an important trend in the macroenvironment. This is contrasted with a thought experiment that envisions the same company having a "do-over" that in this case employs the PLSM approach. This example is the *Everycloud* case.

CHAPTER 11

The *Everycloud* Case

It is generally recognized that effective learning can result from observing how NOT to do something. *Chapter 11* introduces an example from industry of a novel product idea and launch that went wrong. The reasons for its failure may be understood as a lack of an intentional strategy as well as an incoherent implementation.

Cloud-based infrastructure and applications is becoming ubiquitous in industry today. However, 30 years ago, there was a time when the idea of the cloud was only a concept. One such telecommunications company with a wide array of information technology capabilities invested heavily in delivering new services to the public. A small technology department set up a centralized server in the department. Eventually, other departments became aware of this server, so the team added to its capacity, and in addition, it began adding virtual servers so that the server grew to more than just a box for storing data. It became a platform for other departments to use. In essence, the box became the beginnings of a private cloud. Eventually, the cloud became increasingly used throughout the company and was assigned a staff and annual budget to maintain. While this represented a cost to the company, there were clear savings associated with investing in what became a group of servers rather than continuing to invest in desktops, servers, personal computers, and applications throughout the company. Also, the virtual applications, services, and storage "earned" fees from other company departments and divisions through budget chargeback schemes. After 3 years of sustained growth and improvements in what was initially little more than a back-office "Skunk Works" project, one of the team members who founded and championed the server initiated the idea of offering this type of virtual storage and applications to customers. The project was after all working well internally. Why not then offer similar services to paying customers? While such an idea appears natural and intuitive during an era of widespread cloud usage—at the time—offering such services was viewed as a novel idea and met with initial resistance. After ongoing lobbying to offer this as a product to consumers, eventually it was agreed to pilot the concept. It was then that *Everycloud* was born.

Launching *Everycloud*

Before the rise of the cloud, cloud applications, storage, and servers were a rather abstract and conceptual sale. Potential customers who could make use of such a product were not likely to be aware that they needed it—at least initially. A primary candidate for such a product was an existing client who already made extensive purchases of telecommunications products and services. The *Everycloud* founder and champion created educational materials for key account salespeople. Potential anchor customers were then identified, and the product champion joined sales at key client engagements to make the pitch and explain the new product idea. Eventually, one major client decided that the idea was a good one and the first trial of the innovative *Everycloud* product began. The client found the appeal in the bundling of telecommunications connectivity with access to the services that *Everycloud* offered. This is consistent with the old saying that "the less you know about something, the more attractive it appears." In the case of *Everycloud*, the attractive appearance appealed to the company and customer alike. Soon, however, the shortcomings of the organically developed ad hoc product and strategy began to make itself apparent.

No Silver Linings

Once the product found a home with an anchor customer, excitement grew among major account salespeople. This was a means to secure additional revenue from customers. Furthermore, once customers became familiar with the *Everycloud* ecosystem, it would be difficult to change back to running and managing their own infrastructure. Additionally, competition for this type of novel product concept was limited. This in effect gave salespeople the opportunity to further "lock in" major accounts. On the other hand, there was the danger that news about the novel product experiment would soon leak out leading to the growth of competition. The danger was just as high in the case of bad news about product performance leaking out. This not only attracted competitors, but it had the risk of leading customers to consider alternative companies and solutions. After several customers signed up for the service, clouds began brewing on the horizon. The core competence required for building and maintaining telecommunications connectivity is not exactly the same as maintaining cloud services. Different clients have different cloud usage patterns. Some cloud usage is highly resource intensive. At the same time, other cloud clients may require less resources but immediate and highly time-constrained access. A mix of high-resource and immediate demand access clients could set off a perfect storm of contention for scarce cloud resources. This is especially concerning with a new product within a new market, where capacity requirements and client service mix are uncertain. What happened next was that some clients with resource-intensive applications began "bogging down" and crawling through application execution when such applications previously ran quickly. Further, when some clients demanded immediate access, sometimes they were forced to wait while *Everycloud* served other clients. Complaints ensued, and some clients who were currently buying significant volumes of telecommunications connectivity began to threaten to withhold payment until the issues were resolved. The company then attempted to resolve the issues by updating *Everycloud* capacity, connectivity, and processing power. Promises were made and the roll-out of the upgrades ensued. It was soon determined that the mix of requirements arising from new clients required the most advanced hardware and latest releases of software. Upgrading to "bleeding-edge" specifications led *Everycloud* vulnerable to outages and security concerns.

Stakeholder Pushback

Everycloud originated in a technology department that was responsible for developing telecommunication products and services to be offered to the general public. As the internal product expanded and was offered outside of the company, the resentment of the corporate information technology department grew. As *Everycloud* expanded internally,the Information Technology (IT) department felt that this was out of bounds for the technology department and should rightly be offered and supported by IT. Also, the concept itself was viewed as a threat to its power-base of legacy hardware, applications, and systems. Finally, as far as the IT department was concerned, this was a service that no department outside of IT should be offering to the public. The stumbles of *Everycloud* as it expanded triggered IT to lead the charge against *Everycloud*. The product after all was being developed, offered, and maintained by a team perceived to be amateurs in the eyes of IT. Further, the outages, and especially the security concerns, were trumpeted throughout the organization as problems that had the potential to bring down the company. The increasing noise promoted by the IT department along with customer complaints and threats to the core businesses became the "last straw" for executives. The *Everycloud* product development and sales team was ordered to begin adopting new security features as well as several standards viewed as essential by the IT department. The updates to the product were not viewed favorably by customers. The system became so secure that even authorized clients had difficulty accessing the system. The new system pronounced to be "production ready" was more expensive, more complicated than originally sold, and with poorer performance. Further, since IT took control, the system was taken down more often for updates and security patches to be implemented. Customers with an international presence found that late night updates in North America were bringing down an essential service during business hours in Asia and Europe. Instead of IT "saving the day," the situation grew more dire. Executives attending an industry trade show heard public expressions of concern and doubt about the new product. One key customer surreptitiously had the system ported to a competitor's network and cloud system and cancelled significant telecommunication service contracts. The leading industry newspaper published an article about the *Everycloud* "folly." Following this, the industry standards body took up an initiative for standardization of cloud services. The technologies "designed in" to the standard came from a cloud technology offered by a major competitor. The increasing noise level from the industry, major clients, employees, and standards bodies brought the issue to the board of directors. The CEO of the company was strongly encouraged to terminate *Everycloud*. *Everycloud* was indeed terminated, along with the vice president of the division who sponsored the product.

What Went Wrong?

The irony of this scenario is that months after the termination of *Everycloud*, cloud services began to pop up throughout the marketplace with offerings from players such as Amazon, Google, and Microsoft. A potential windfall of a new business launched at the earliest days of the virtualization of servers and the cloud was abruptly ended just when the market was becoming ready for such a concept. What was observed to be a bold move full of risks at the time is now in retrospect commonplace and something for which the company should have followed through and driven to the point where it was a success. The story of *Everycloud* is by no means unusual. In fact, it is a familiar story that has played out many times with many technologies over the years. To name but a few examples:

1. Kodak and digital photography
   Kodak was a company that enjoyed huge revenues and profits from the film business within the camera industry. Like *Everycloud*, Kodak management encountered new technologies that tended to "bubble up" through the organization. One such organic technology was digital photography. Early digital photography did not work nearly as well as film. Investment in digital photography required to make it equivalent in performance of film was huge. Further, the effort to arrive at a time when a new market for such a product was years away. When and if it did arrive, it had the potential to end the film business. From the perspective of the senior executive and the directors of the company, what sense would it make to forgo profits by spending heavily in R&D only at the end of the process to kill the nearly 100-year-old "cash cow"? Too many forces opposed the nurture of this technology. However, in the same way as *Everycloud*, the technology did eventually arrive in the marketplace and was delivered by competitors. Further, it did kill the Kodak cash cow. But

the profits associated with the new technology were earned by new-comers to the industry rather than Kodak. PLSM could have offered alternatives by forcing a systematic ongoing analysis of trends and strategies. But at Kodak, and in the *Everycloud* environment, it did not exist.

2. Xerox (and the mouse and the GUI)

   Xerox is known for its copy machines. Xerox thrived when copy machines were the lifeblood of business. As the industry shifted away from its emphasis on paper copies and toward digital media with occasional on-demand printing, the Xerox hold on the now smaller copy machine market began to fade. What is less known is the early innovation of Xerox in the design of the computer GUI (Graphical User Interface). Xerox developed in its Palo Alto Research Center (PARC) a user interface for computers in the early 1970s—far earlier than personal computers became a reality for businesses and consumers. This user interface included elements familiar to us today, including the image of the virtual "desktop," graphics instead of typed commands, and, finally, the mouse. Xerox used the interface in its research center, and visitors to the center were able to see it. The Xerox GUI influenced early computers—particularly Apple. While Xerox later introduced a workstation product that incorporated the interface, it was late to the game and missed the rise of the personal computer market. Could the vision of the Xerox graphical user interface have been realized had Xerox employed a process and project management approach to vetting and developing new designs and technologies? Rather than an aging copy machine company, perhaps Xerox could have become the Apple, Dell, or Lenovo of today.

3. Blockbuster Video and Media Distribution

   It has been said that companies that define themselves with sufficient breadth have an improved chance of surviving in the face of techno-logical and macroenvironmental change. For example, a passenger railroad may not survive in an era of automobiles, buses, and airlines but may survive if defined as a transportation company rather than a railroad. Blockbuster may be a victim of narrow definition along with the shortsightedness that limited its ability to envision media consumption technologies of the future. Is it possible that a company with an intensive and closely managed strategic management process may have been alerted earlier to the shifts in media distribution technologies—and adapted before it was too late? While this is only a matter of speculation, it is likely that a closely managed and governed strategic management system would lead to greater visibility to shifts in the macroenvironment.

An interesting aspect of products such as *Everycloud* is that they were unplanned; organic; bottom-up efforts that began small, grew big, and then "just happened." The strategic import of such a product was therefore missed. In essence, *Everycloud* is an example of an emergent strategy that in this case—and in many others—did not emerge leading to the consequences of a failed strategy and missed opportunity. Could the combination of project and strategic management have made a difference? To follow is an alternative *Everycloud* scenario—the one that did not happen—and the one that may have had a silver lining had it emerged under the umbrella of project management–led strategic planning.

Could the Clouds Have Parted?

Consider a different scenario where the company employed a strategic planning cycle using project management to produce strategic deliverables at every junction of the process. Imagine further that the company governed a strategic planning and management process that:

1. Solicited new product development proposals
2. Vetted and funded product development and innovation proposals
3. Governed the product development process by:
   a. Chartering projects for each component of strategic planning
   b. Chartering projects for implementing products associated with strategic initiatives
   c. Made ongoing "Go/No-Go" strategic business decisions at each strategy and product development milestone.

What would *Everycloud* have become in such an environment? Would there have been a silver lining (Figure 35)?

Everycloud: Ad hoc versus PLSM

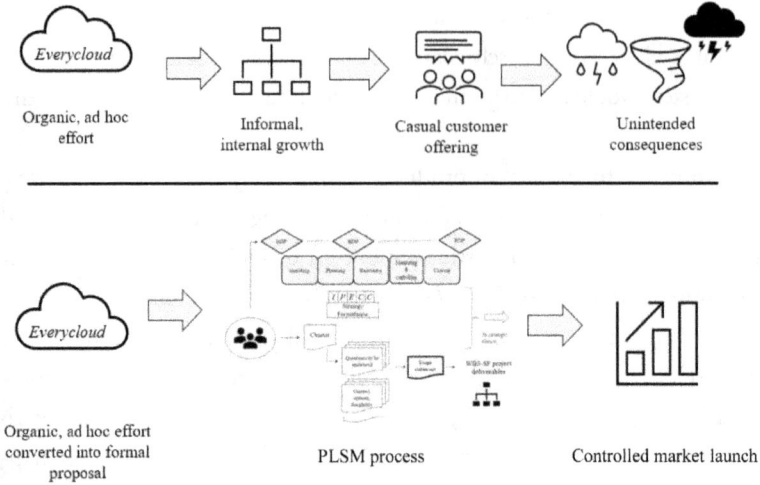

| Organic, ad hoc effort | Informal, internal growth | Casual customer offering | Unintended consequences |

| Organic, ad hoc effort converted into formal proposal | PLSM process | Controlled market launch |

Figure 35 *Everycloud ad hoc versus PLSM*

CHAPTER 12

The *Everycloud* Alternative History

What would a product launch as well as a strategic implementation failure look like if things were done differently? Chapter 12 describes what the process-focused alternative to ad hoc methods could have been. The benefits of closely managed processes and "planning before doing" are observed to pay off.

A senior manager within the technology department of a large telecommunication company took notice that the backroom "server" tool developed for departmental use had begun to explode in demand as other departments began to employ the technology for use in carrying out their work. This increasing activity was observed to reduce department infrastructure. The senior manager further noticed that, in spite of the addition of a dedicated team to manage the ever-growing server, it reduced the overall costs of hardware and application licensing due to the new virtualization technology. The success of what was once just an afterthought then led to the determination that this server is something that customers of the company's telecommunication services may find useful. This thought triggered the creation of a new product proposal to present to the governing body for strategic initiatives and new products—the company PAC or "Product Approval Committee."

The Proposal Pt. 1

The senior manager presented a proposal for a new service to be offered to key clients beginning with a pilot run. To emphasize the power of virtualization, the new product proposal was christened *Everycloud*. After consideration of the proposal, the product approval committee observed that chartered strategic projects were nearing the end of the analysis phase. The committee suggested that the *Everycloud* decision be tabled for 30 days in order to evaluate the outcome of strategic analysis. It was further directed that within 2 weeks, the interim findings of the strategic analysis project be shared with the *Everycloud* team. The team would then be requested to evaluate the *Everycloud* product in terms of its alignment with trends identified by the strategic analysis project. The *Everycloud* team was then requested to revisit the existing problem with substantial additional work related to alignment with strategic trends. Upon review of the proposal in 30 days, the product approval committee would issue a "Go/No-Go" decision on the proposal. It was further decided that the *Everycloud* team would be provided with an additional budget to continue for the next 30 days in analyzing and developing the proposal.

The Proposal Pt. 2

The *Everycloud* team began the presentation after the next product approval committee meeting was called to order. The team presented the original rationale for the product including the story of its rapid internal growth within the company. The team then proceeded to identify alignments of the project with the interim results of the strategic analysis project. The key points of alignment included the following observations:

1. The trend toward outsourcing IT infrastructure and software continued to grow rapidly.
2. The increasing focus on the use of virtual machines paired with low-cost hardware and storage would likely lead to market adoption of *Everycloud*-like products in one form or another.
3. With the continued growth of IP-based communications, evidence exists that current or potential telecommunication customers are consolidating spending of telecommunications and IT within a single budget.

The product approval committee asked several questions and then adjourned for the purpose of considering the proposal. Upon returning from the closed conference, the proposal was approved as a pilot project contingent upon the identification of an anchor customer. It was also requested by the executive committee that *Everycloud* be promoted extensively within the company in order to fully exercise the application, thoroughly vet it, and address identified issues prior to launching with the trial anchor customer. The executive team assigned resources and funding for 3 months to authorize the team to develop a detailed plan and take the product through additional internal trials. Further, the product approval committee assigned core team members from sales and marketing, information technology, and operations so that the plan included a holistic view of product requirements. The next PAC review was then scheduled 3 months later—or sooner if necessary, in the case of the team finding that it was going beyond planned scope, schedule, and budget constraints assigned by the committee.

Plan Review

The *Everycloud* team appeared before the product approval committee to present the complete plan for the product launch. The presentation began with the identification of the anchor customer along with a risk management plan to ensure that any problems arising from the pilot launch did not impact current business with the company nor damage relationships in any way. Two key mitigation efforts were proposed to counter any ill effects to existing business. The first was establishing a hotline for customer direct access to the *Everycloud* project manager at any time a problem arose. The second mitigation effort was a key component of the communication plan. Each week a status update meeting would be held between the customer and the *Everycloud* product team. A project team member would be present at the customer site every other meeting to provide oversight of ongoing issues.

In keeping with the holistic arrangement of having all key functions represented on the project core team, the project manager presented a comprehensive update including the sales and marketing view, the financial perspective, the update from operations, and, finally, a proposal from the IT core team member. IT had provided input on security concerns. The project team had "pushed back" against the recommendations due to the observation that uptime and performance guarantees would likely not be able to be maintained. The project manager discussed a proposal for enhancing security while, at the same time, minimizing the possibility of performance concerns. All core team members signed off on the proposal and in doing so set the stage for buy-in across all functional groups within the company. After a question and answer period, the product approval committee members went into closed session to confer on the pros and cons of greenlighting the plan in light of identified risks and mitigation strategies. The committee returned from the conference and called the meeting to order once again. *Everycloud* was a go.

Pilot Program Closure and Lessons Learned

While issues arose during the pilot run, the mitigation plans put in place acted quickly to smooth over issues and prevent them escalating into serious problems. The proposed security measures functioned with few incidents and with little impact on operational performance. During the pilot run, the customer identified several shortcomings in the product and created a prioritized wish list for future releases. The identified issues were adapted into a set of requirements for *Everycloud* 2.0. Finally, at the end of the pilot, the client requested that the pilot product be evolved into a fully commercial platform with *Everycloud* service discounts provided in return for continued evaluation and ongoing vetting of the product. An agreement was reached to this end.

The *Everycloud* project team presented a lessons learned review of the project and itemized the completed closure checklist. Prior to the end of the project closure presentation, the project team presented a proposal for *Everycloud* 2.0 and its launch as a commercial product geared to the market at large. The core team member representing sales and marketing presented a synopsis of comments from the pilot client, other potential clients, as well as positive industry buzz that had arisen from the *Everycloud* trial. The concept of cloud service offerings appeared to be gaining wide acceptance given the rise of virtualization. It was becoming recognized that standards may need to be in place to foster this industry. The path pioneered by *Everycloud* provided a technology road map that appeared sufficiently sound to become the basis of future standards. The *Everycloud* architecture, as a result, had been presented to the primary industry standards body for consideration in developing an industry standard. . It was further noted that the incorporation of the *Everycloud* architecture into the standard could likely lead to additional revenues derived from licensing agreements from competitors. The product approval committee after closed conference and conferral accepted the project closure and lessons learned documentation and approved the charter for *Everycloud* 2.0. It was also observed that by this time, the strategic planning cycle had nearly completed the strategy formulation project. The documentation was requested to be filed into the appropriate area for life cycle documentation and made available for the strategy formulation team for consideration. It was also concluded that the success of this development and pilot project would be weighed heavily during the strategic choice project and business decision-making meeting. The backroom "skunkworks" project had taken root by means of a systematic approach to project life cycle and project-led strategic management. *Everycloud* would become a key offering that hinted at a renewed future of market leadership.

Everycloud Epilog

Five years after chartering *Everycloud* 2.0, a few of the members of the original team are in the audience of an industry conference listening to the state of the industry.

> There are a few key players in today's cloud services industry. While this new approach to managing infrastructure and applications is relatively new, one player stands out as the leader in innovation within this market. Everycloud takes the number one position and continues to have the dominant market share. The volume of business has led to the spinoff of the Everycloud product line as its own company—a wholly owned subsidiary of the sponsoring parent company. This bold move into cloud services came at the right time as revenues from traditional IT and telecommunications services have continued to dwindle over time. The industry however benefits from competition, so many industry analysts are standing by to see possible future responses from the Microsoft, Amazons, or even the Googles of the world

The original *Everycloud* team could not help but smile. It was time to head to the lobby bar and propose a toast recognizing the good fortune of working for a process-focused company that practiced Project-Led Strategic Management.

CHAPTER 13

Project-Led Strategic Management (PLSM): Summarizing Core Elements

One of the challenges of any process-focused management methodology is the tendency for managers to struggle with the large number of supporting processes. As an example, the PMBOK includes 49 such processes supporting the management of projects. One way to gain comfort with using a process framework is to seek to distill the processes into its essential underlying principles. Chapter 13 provides a summary of the key principles along with contrasting approaches to strategic management so that the methodology may be intuitively appreciated.

The information age in which the industry of today inhabits is a fast-moving kaleidoscope of constant change and often confusing signals. Like the ship in the storm navigating to the nearest waypoint, a company to be successful and to attain and maintain a competitive advantage must have the equivalent of a compass, a sextant, along with a captain who knows how to use it. The internal compass is a structured framework that offers a systematic means for navigating through the winds and rolling seas while staying on course. The following key observations are therefore proposed:

1. Structuring the strategic management process can be a significant vehicle for enterprise navigation in the chaotic information age.
2. Successful leaders avoid viewing the strategic work of the firm as a continuous process and instead are able to detect the series of steps involved as well as the discrete nature of accomplishing goals, arriving at waypoints, and controlling the progress of producing discrete deliverables.
3. Developing the strategy of the company and successfully implementing it is as complex a series of discrete iterative steps as any challenging large-scale system development project.

4. Project management processes developed for closely managing the production of discrete, unique, high-risk deliverables uniquely fit the steps involved in strategic analysis, formulation, choice, and implementation.

5. Far from constraining creativity and intuition, project-led strategic management (PLSM) focuses attention on those things that matter most to company executives. (This is preferred over the alternative of continually attempting to decide what to do, when to do it, and how to do it.) An executive mind freed from the stresses of process uncertainty is now able to focus on the goal of finding the best ground in which to fight—and uncovering the means for the unfair advantage.

PLSM: An Illustration in Contrasts

Insights on how to view and appreciate the benefits of PLSM can be readily observed by contrasting with a typical alternative—the application of ad hoc methods. When each phase of strategic planning is evaluated with respect to the application of ad hoc versus using the structured approach of PLSM, significant differences are observed, as shown in Tables 4 to 8.

Table 4 Overall Management of Strategic Planning

Ad Hoc Methods	PLSM
Processes employed not clearly stated or documented.	Clear processes employed and documented.
Overall goals of strategic planning are not clearly understood.	The goal of seeking a competitive "unfair advantage" is clearly stated and strongly reinforced.
Strategic planning and implementation lack a clear framework and cycle and are often triggered by events.	Strategic planning and implementation are governed from the top of the organization using an intentional schedule and implementation framework.
Ad hoc methods rely on the heroics of individual contributors who come and go over time.	Relies on following, maintaining, and optimizing a process in order to focus the attention and funding of the firm and to achieve repeatable results.

Table 5 Strategic Analysis

Ad Hoc Methods	PLSM
Analysis tends to focus on recent events and triggers without clear strategic intent.	Strategic analysis is focused on clear goals outlined in the analysis project charter.
Strategic analysis is often carried out by various individuals and is loosely managed.	Strategic analysis is closely managed using project management practices.

Table 6 Strategic Formulation

Ad Hoc Methods	PLSM
Formulated strategies are often operational and tactical in focus and strongly weighted toward current events and incremental change.	The formulation of strategy is a carefully weighed outcome based on data from the analysis project, theoretical models, internal capabilities, and with the goal of the unfair advantage in mind.

Table 7 Strategic Choice

Ad Hoc Methods	PLSM
Strategies are selected based on opinion, intuition, or political landscape of the company.	Strategies are selected by employing rigorous qualitative and quantitative techniques adopted from project management practices.
The decision to explicitly select a strategy may be deferred or ignored—thereby leading to the "strategy" of the status quo.	The decision to explicitly select a strategy is recognized as being an important responsibility that cannot be deferred. Strategic decisions are made following the strategy formulation project.
Strategic decisions are soft tacit decisions rather than hard explicit decisions. They may not be widely communicated nor widely known by the employees of the company.	Strategic decisions are explicitly made, widely communicated, and published. Employees are aware of the strategy and are able to communicate it.

Table 8 Strategic Implementation

Ad Hoc Methods	PLSM
Strategy may not be sufficient clear to be executed effectively.	Strategy is clearly articulated facilitating implementation.
Strategy lacks operational clarity and SMART goals.	Strategy is stated in terms of SMART objectives and executed by charting implementation projects.
Top-level strategies are rarely linked to clear, measurable operational metrics.	Top-level strategies are linked to operational constructs, chartered as projects, and monitored by the ongoing measurement of KPIs.
Top-level strategies are communicated in a general way to the functional groups of the organization.	Top-level strategies are broken down into strategic initiative projects and formally chartered to closely manage implementation.
The implementation of strategy is weakly pursued with little follow-up (or follow-through).	Strategy implementation is governed by the strong oversight of strategic implementation projects governed by the executive oversight or PAC (Product or Project Approval Committee).

PLSM: Final Takeaways

The contrast between ad hoc methods and PLSM within strategic planning and implementation is striking. On the one hand is the company that is pushed in different directions by the ebb and flow of changes in the macroenvironment, the efforts of individuals, and perhaps the internal political landscape. In such a company, "strategy happens" but often what happens is not strategy. A company making the decision to employ PLSM may not know which direction to go—but will have a clear process for figuring this out. PLSM is a framework for becoming intentional, seeking the clear goal of the unfair advantage, closely managing the work of arriving at a strategy, and, finally, carefully governing the implementation of strategy. Finally, the challenging, intangible, and mentally challenging exercise of deciding which way to go along with how and when is broken into tangible bites using ready-made project management methods that have thrived in equally demanding but different environments. PLSM is not "trying and hoping for the best," it is "doing" and succeeding.

References

Benefits Realization Management. 2019.

Doran, G.T. 1981. "There's A SMART Way to Write Management's Goals and Objectives." *Management Review* 70, no. 11, pp. 35-6.

Drucker, P.F. 1995. *People and Performance: The Best of Peter Drucker on Management*. London, England: Routledge.

Governance of Portfolios, Programs, and Projects: A Practice Guide. 2016.

Holsapple, C. (Ed.). 2013. *Handbook on Knowledge Management 1: Knowledge Matters* (Vol. 1). Berlin, Germany: Springer Science & Business Media.

Implementing Organizational Project Management: A Practice Guide. 2014.

Kaplan, R.S., and D.P. Norton. 2005. "The Balanced Scorecard: Measures That Drive Performance." *Harvard Business Review*, 83, no. 7, p. 172.

Kaplan, R.S., and D.P. Norton. 1996. "Using the Balanced Scorecard as a Strategic Management System." *Harvard Business Review*, 85, no. 7.

Kaplan, R.S., and D.P. Norton. (1996). "Linking the Balanced Scorecard to Strategy." *California Management Review*, 39, no. 1, pp. 53-79.

Kim, W.C., and R. Mauborgne. 2014. *Blue Ocean Strategy Expanded Edition: How to Create Uncontested Market Space and Make the Competition Irrelevant*. Boston, MA: Harvard Business Review Press.

Kim, W.C., and R. Mauborgne. 2014. "Blue Ocean Leadership." *Harvard Business Review*, 92, no. 5, pp. 60-72.

Kim, W.C. 2005. "Blue Ocean Strategy: From Theory to Practice." *California Management Review*, 47, no. 3, pp. 105-21.

PMBOK® Guide—Sixth Edition. 2017.

Porter, M.E. 2008. "The Five Competitive Forces That Shape Strategy." *Harvard Business Review*, 86, no. 1, pp. 25-40.

Porter, M.E. 1989. How competitive forces shape strategy. In *Readings in Strategic Management* (pp. 133-143). London, England: Palgrave.

Porter, M.E., and M.R. Kramer. 2002. "The Competitive Advantage of Corporate Philanthropy." *Harvard Business Review*, 80, no. 12, pp. 56-68.

Porter, M.E. 1997. "Competitive Strategy." *Measuring Business Excellence*, 1, pp. 12-7.

Porter, M.E. 2011. *Competitive Advantage of Nations: Creating and Sustaining Superior Performance*. New York, NY: Simon and Schuster.

Reeves, M., S. Moose, and T. Venema. 2014. *The Growth Share Matrix*. BCG–The Boston Consulting Group.

Sull, D.N. 2007. "Closing the Gap Between Strategy and Execution." *MIT Sloan Management Review*, 48, no. 4, pp. 30-8.

The Standard for Earned Value Management. 2019.

The Standard for Organizational Project Management. 2018.

The Standard for Program Management—Fourth Edition. 2017.

The Standard for Portfolio Management—Third Edition. 2013.

The Standard for Portfolio Management—Fourth Edition. 2017.

About the Authors

Dr. James W. Marion is a tenured associate professor with Embry-Riddle Aeronautical University-Worldwide. He is currently the chair of the Department of Decision Sciences in the College of Business. His experience includes leading large organizations in multiple project launches in the United States, Europe, and Asia. Dr. Marion has a PhD in organization and management with specialization in information technology management from Capella University. He has an MS in engineering from the University of Wisconsin-Platteville and an MSc and MBA in strategic planning as well as a postgraduate certificate in business research methods from The Edinburgh Business School of Heriot-Watt University. He is a certified project management professional (PMP).

Dr. John Lewis is a developer, system architect, and computer enthusiast who has, since an early age, been keenly interested in electronics. John is currently a lead member of architecture at AT&T, where over the past 30 years he has received more than 100 U.S. patents on his ideas in the communications field. He attended the State Technical Institute in Memphis, Grantham College of Engineering, and the then Memphis State University.

Dr. Tracey Richardson is a tenured associate professor of project management in the College of Business at Embry-Riddle Aeronautical University-Worldwide. While serving in the United States Air Force, over more than 20 years, Dr. Richardson had the opportunity to visit more than 20 countries, and more than half of the United States, managing the same challenges in operations and logistics, aircraft maintenance, backshop manufacturing, and sortie management and facing them with limited resources and regulation encountered by global companies.

Dr. Richardson has a doctorate in organizational leadership from Argosy University's School of Psychology; she earned her master's degree in management and bachelor of science degree in resource management from Troy University. She is a certified project management professional and a Project Management Institute (PMI) risk management professional.

Index

OTHER TITLES IN OUR PORTFOLIO AND PROJECT MANAGEMENT COLLECTION

Timothy Kloppenborg, *Editor*

- *A.G.I.L.E. Thinking Demystified* by Frank Forte
- *Discoveries Through Personal Agility* by Raji Sivaraman and Michal Raczka
- *Project Communications: A Critical Factor for Project Success* by Connie Plowman and Jill Diffendal
- *Quantitative Tools of Project Management* by David L. Olson
- *The People Project Triangle: Balancing Delivery, Business-as-Usual, and People's Welfare* by Stuart Copeland and Andy Coaton
- *How to Fail at Change Management: A Manager's Guide to the Pitfalls of Managing Change* by James Marion and John Lewis
- *Core Concepts of Project Management* by David L. Olson
- *Projects, Programs, and Portfolios in Strategic Organizational Transformation* by James Jiang and Gary Klein
- *Capital Project Management, Volume I: Capital Project Strategy* by Robert N. McGrath
- *Capital Project Management, Volume II: Capital Project Finance* by Robert N. McGrath
- *Capital Project Management, Volume III: Evolutionary Forces* by Robert N. McGrath
- *Executing Global Projects: A Practical Guide to Applying the PMBOK Framework in the Global Environment* by James Marion and Tracey Richardson
- *Project Communication from Start to Finish: The Dynamics of Organizational Success* by Geraldine E. Hynes
- *The Lost Art of Planning Projects* by Louise Worsley and Christopher Worsley
- *Project Portfolio Management, Second Edition: A Model for Improved Decision Making* by Clive N. Enoch

Concise and Applied Business Books

The Collection listed above is one of 30 business subject collections that Business Expert Press has grown to make BEP a premiere publisher of print and digital books. Our concise and applied books are for…

- Professionals and Practitioners
- Faculty who adopt our books for courses
- Librarians who know that BEP's Digital Libraries are a unique way to offer students ebooks to download, not restricted with any digital rights management
- Executive Training Course Leaders
- Business Seminar Organizers

Business Expert Press books are for anyone who needs to dig deeper on business ideas, goals, and solutions to everyday problems. Whether one print book, one ebook, or buying a digital library of 110 ebooks, we remain the affordable and smart way to be business smart. For more information, please visit **www.businessexpertpress.com**, or contact **sales@businessexpertpress.com**.

www.ingramcontent.com/pod-product-compliance
Lightning Source LLC
Chambersburg PA
CBHW061328220326
41599CB00026B/5090